May you find a strong
will to guide you in life

Blessings,

Marcia Wright

STRONG WILL

His Journey

Marcia Wright

WESTBOW
PRESS®
A DIVISION OF THOMAS NELSON
& ZONDERVAN

Scripture quotations marked NIV are taken from The Holy Bible, New
International Version®, NIV® Copyright © 1973, 1978, 1984, 2011 by
Biblica, Inc.® Used by permission. All rights reserved worldwide.

Scripture quotations marked KJV are taken from the King James Version.

Scripture quotations marked AMP are taken from the Amplified® Bible,
Copyright © 2015 by The Lockman Foundation. Used by permission.

WestBow Press books may be ordered through booksellers or by contacting:

WestBow Press
A Division of Thomas Nelson & Zondervan
1663 Liberty Drive
Bloomington, IN 47403
www.westbowpress.com
1 (866) 928-1240

ISBN: 978-1-9736-6073-6 (sc)
ISBN: 978-1-9736-6074-3 (hc)
ISBN: 978-1-9736-6075-0 (e)

Library of Congress Control Number: 2019904640

Print information available on the last page.

WestBow Press rev. date: 05/14/2019

For Bill
and those who have the privilege
of loving deeply

FOREWORD

Pancreatic cancer affects nice people who have taken good care of themselves and are often looking forward to the joys of time with family, friends, and the flexibility that characterizes retirement. Pancreatic cancer has no racial or ethnic bias and seems to occur at the most inconvenient time. It is a multisystem disease that often causes high blood sugar levels, challenges with maintaining weight and nutritional health, and frequent doctor visits for bile duct stents, CT scans, chemotherapy, radiation therapy, and surgery. The diagnosis of pancreatic cancer is frightening and treatment can be exhausting – reactions which are both understandable and, importantly, modifiable by caring and dedicated treatment teams. Successful treatment requires a team – doctors, nurse practitioners, physician assistants, dieticians, diabetes management specialists, psychologists and many more. Patients and their families should seek out a team that can comprehensively care for their physical and emotional needs while providing the best and most innovative oncologic care. Such innovative care is delivered by physicians and scientists who bring discoveries from the laboratory bench to the patient's bedside. New treatments made available through access to carefully constructed clinical trials offer hope for the patients of today. The inquisitive minds of committed physicians and scientists will insure that we have even better treatments for the patients of tomorrow. Faith, family and a dedicated medical team are invaluable as courageous patients experience both joy and sadness. Marcia Wright provides the "strong will" needed to navigate those challenging times when sadness fills more of the horizon than we all would like. Her carefully chosen words offer hope – what every cancer patient is looking for!

Douglas B. Evans, M.D.
Professor and Chair
Department of Surgery
Medical College of Wisconsin
Milwaukee, Wisconsin

Pancreatic cancer is a challenging disease. It alters the lives of our patients and their families and presents an ongoing obstacle to the healthcare givers who seek to understand and defeat it. We are honored to meet the brave and enduring patients and their families who come to us with this disease. Bill and his wife, Marcia, are one such special pair. Together they were a united force. They traveled far from the comforts of home, seeking specialized medical care, with the hope of a better chance at combating this disease. They found our team at the Medical College of Wisconsin. We fought with them with every tool and strategy possible to make Bill's cancer, history. Despite months of prior chemotherapy, Bill was brave in facing into concurrent chemotherapy and radiation. Marcia was his strongest ally, with endless emotional and physical encouragement and support. Such love and support are life giving, and a tool that can improve prognosis. Despite his own cancer journey, Bill was willing to participate in a clinical trial where his tumor was imaged once per week on a Linear accelerator with an MRI unit (MR-Linac). Hidden within these images, perhaps, are some clues that will tell us if our patients are responding to radiation and chemotherapy during their weeks of radiation. His generosity in contributing to the fund of knowledge for future patients is one that we are most grateful for. The story of Bill and Marcia is a testimony in courage and perseverance and the power of love and faith while experiencing the challenges of illness. We are honored to have been a part of this journey and only wish that it could have been more victorious for Bill and Marcia. We know that Bill's contributions to our knowledge will help future patients who we are fighting for even before we meet them.

Beth Erickson, MD, FACR,FASTRO, FABR
Radiation Oncologist
Medical College of Wisconsin
Milwaukee, Wisconsin

Our family: Zac, Jenn, Marcia, Bill, and Aaron

PREFACE

Originally, this book was a journal intended to update friends and family about my husband, Bill's, progress as he received treatment for pancreatic cancer. The diagnosis came mid-October of 2017 and by November we launched a Caring Bridge© website with the help of my sister, Linda. It was a way to post the most recent updates about Bill's care and treatment and make sure everyone had the same information in a timely manner. What came of it, though, was a remarkable walk of faith, testimony, strength and courage. Bill survived ten months. He gave it his all fighting hard against a terrible cancer. Through these many months we cried and worried and prayed and shared these concerns with our Caring Bridge© followers who were steadfast in their support and encouragement. It became a virtual lifeline.

The journal entries in this book are chronological. Following my entries are a few of the comments from friends and family who followed our journey. We started with a visit to Milwaukee, Wisconsin where we met a surgeon, Dr. Douglas Evans, whose diligent efforts to find treatment for pancreatic cancer gave us hope. The plan was to prepare Bill for surgery and removal of the tumor. This surgery required many intricate aspects in order for it to be successful. Not only did Bill receive heavy duty doses of chemotherapy in Michigan (directed by Dr. Jeffrey Margolis at Beaumont Hospital's Rose Cancer Center), he had radiation supported by additional chemotherapy and masterfully orchestrated by Dr. Beth Erickson, radiation oncologist at the Medical College of Wisconsin. Dr. Erickson's goal was to shrink the cancer from the vasculature around the pancreas and make it possible for Dr. Evans to surgically excise the tumor. Even with this very complicated procedure, it is not a "sure thing." The cancer often returns. But we hoped to extend Bill's life and have more time together. We moved from our home in Michigan to Wisconsin for almost six months to receive this treatment and for Bill to have the surgery and follow up care while there. Unfortunately, the last CT scan before the scheduled surgery showed metastasis to the liver. That eliminated surgery. We tried more chemotherapy and investigated a clinical trial in Arizona. None of these options proved fruitful and Bill's health declined. He died August 4, 2018 at a Hospice Home in our hometown in Michigan.

At that point, most people who use Caring Bridge© cease their entries and deactivate the site. For me though, I was compelled to continue to share. Bill's story became our love story. We were implicitly connected through all of this and though I was the writer, I was able to share some of Bill's thoughts along with mine. It became part of the story of <u>our</u> lives. The responses on Caring Bridge © were insightful testimonies of faith and it occurred to me (through the urging of friends and family) our story might be helpful to others experiencing similar circumstances. From that "Strong Will" was created. May you find peace, comfort, companionship and God's love in these words.

Marcia Wright

2 Irishmen toast to hope- Bill with Aaron

A Miracle in Progress

November 16, 2017

After we received a grim diagnosis for Bill's pancreatic cancer, we felt defeated and hopeless. Bill's Michigan oncologist told us about a doctor in Milwaukee who was making some gains in the area of pancreatic cancer. So we went to meet with him. His amazing opinion was that with chemo and radiation he can surgically remove the tumor in several months. We are so grateful and know the prayers of many are being answered!

> *Marcia and Bill, we want you to know that you are in our thoughts and prayers. God bless you both as you go through this journey. Hugs for you both.*
>
> —*Your neighbors, Tom and Julie*

Chemo #2

November 28, 2017

We went to Beaumont Hospital's Rose Cancer Center where Bill received chemotherapy and treatment. After six tough hours of infusions we headed to a local hotel where we will stay for a couple of days and see how Bill tolerates the chemo. He will return to the Cancer Center in two days to get his pump disconnected and then home with a patch on his arm for another 24 hours. It's a whole week of chemo in many different forms. Right now he is resting. Pizza, oddly, hit the spot for dinner. I say, "We take it. Whatever sounds good is what we will have!"

> *Marcia, you and Bill will continue to be in my prayers. I smiled yesterday as I hung an ornament on my Christmas tree you made me years ago. It is still beautiful! I know God is with you and Bill— may you feel His loving presence.*
>
> *—Diane*

> *Hi neighbors, we are thinking of you both. Bob and I had fun being with you the other night. Keeping you in our prayers, sending love, hugs and positive vibes. You got this!*
>
> *—Cindy M*

> *As always, please give Bill my best. I'll continue to keep you both in my thoughts and prayers with my very best wishes. Make Bill smile and tell him I said "Go Blue!"*
>
> *—Karen P*

> *So proud of how God is using you both as such great ambassadors! Stay strong, keep your chin up, and look for ways to continue to be such a blessing to those He has put in your path!*
>
> *—Sally R*

The Sun Is Shining

December 1, 2017

This morning the sun is shining literally and in our hearts. Bill said "I feel really good today! The best I've felt since before the diagnosis." Amazing—it is a chemo week and at the end of it he feels better! If that isn't God responding to the prayers of many, I don't know what is. Feeling thankful for these miracles along the way.

> *Eureka! Best news with weather to match. Enjoy these moments of sun and good feelings.*
> *—Louann*

> *I was just thinking about all the fun I used to have with you and Bill. It makes my heart feel wonderful to know that Bill is feeling good today. Yes, there is a God and look at the prayers he has sent to bless Bill. Love you both.*
> *—Dianna*

Hills and Valleys

December 5, 2017

Today we are back at Beaumont and Bill is getting IVs to help with fatigue/ nausea/ dehydration. Last night we had a great visit with daughter Jenn and her good friend Lara from Columbus. Bill felt lousy all day but rallied while they were here. Young people have that effect. Given his symptoms the doctor wanted to see him and it was the right thing to do. They tweaked his meds to get the right combination for him. I'm hoping this will help because Bill's mom, sister, and brother-in-law are coming tonight from northern Michigan for a couple of days.

What is it with you two? You never miss a beat and, in fact, add a few to this dance you are involved in. Seems like the visits are going ahead as scheduled. It is all good. Enjoy the upcoming visit with family.

—Louann

May God's love continue to surround you and your family. Blessings. Love. Hugs.

—Lisa D

Family and friend visits are good medicine. Enjoy your company this week. Prayers are continuing for both of you. Take care.

—Cherryl

The Little Things

December 10, 2017

It's funny how a journey like this creates celebrations in silly little ways. Bill feels good today. Hooray! His appetite is normal and he is able to watch the Lions play football without feeling ill. Well, that may be just the impact of the Lions. We know what a trying team they are.

He still avoids being out in crowds to protect his immune system but the snow this week end makes looking outside from a cozy inside pleasant. Tuesday he starts chemo round three and there will be some rough days, but we are hoping for another surge of wellbeing at the end of that time. Thank you all for prayers and good wishes and the "attaboys." It uplifts us both.

> *Continuing our prayers for successful treatment, healing, and peace!*
> *—Cheryll*

> *Attaboy and attagirl!!*
> *—Sue*

> *You are in our thoughts and prayers every day. It is like cheering on a runner in a marathon with a cause. We just quite simply love you and have faith that our prayers are heard. Keep on keeping on.*
> *We are right there with you cheering you on.*
> *—Linda & Jim*

> *Glad you can enjoy some good days before the next round! The snow must look beautiful around the pond. Caring thoughts!*
> *—Julie S*

> *You both are in my prayers daily. What a wonderful reminder for all of us to find the joy in the little things in our lives. Praying for another good day.*
> *—Diane*

And We're Off

December 12, 2017

It's chemo #3 and Bill is resting in a recliner with many IV lines running into his port. But amid all the medical necessities, we are celebrating *another* good day! A ham sandwich on marbled rye tasted great and he's navigating snoozing, texting and visiting with other patients and people who are becoming friends as we make this journey. I've said it before but the simplest happy, comfy responses are so meaningful when there are darker days. An important takeaway: make it all count. Gratitude for pleasures we once took for granted just intensifies God's blessings on us.

We'll stay in town until Thursday and then go home. The snow is picture perfect and it's toasty inside. For this moment, it's enough.

> *Fresh snow plus sun is beautiful, isn't it? Glad you are staying in town. You are in a rhythm right now. Hope it helps a little that you know what to expect within this treatment pattern. Glad there are friendly people around. I'm sending positive vibes your way through cyberspace.*
>
> —*Julie S*

> *Thank you for taking time to keep us all updated on Bill's progress. Prayer warriors are still working overtime!*
>
> —*Sally P*

> *Wishing you both a good day tomorrow! The bad weather that's predicted makes your hotel room sound cozy and inviting.*
>
> —*Sue*

Moment by Moment

December 12, 2017

As great as today's treatment went, nausea, neuropathy, and blacking out are plaguing Bill. He's trying to drink fluids and stay hydrated, but for those of you visiting the site this evening, prayers for healing are appreciated. Thank you all for caring about us.

> *Very tough on you both. Hope morning brings some relief for Bill. You are in our prayers every day.*
>
> *—Julie S*

> *You know you are always in my prayers. I hope tomorrow is a better day.*
>
> *—Barbara*

Snow and Sleep

December 13, 2017

It's beautiful to watch the snow from the window of our hotel. I went out to pick up a prescription and wander the local mall for a bit. Best of all (and here I go again with the little shreds of gratitude) is that Bill slept and slept and slept. Soup from PF Chang's hit the spot and back to bed he went. So grateful for the restorative power of sleep and prayer. As we ease into evening he feels relatively good. Praise God.

> *I love your "attitude of gratitude". It was something my mother always demonstrated and I see that in you. Love you, friend*
>
> *-Linda S*

> *It really takes those small moments to create gratitude!! Love you guys.*
>
> *—Cindy H*

> *Glad that soup and sleep are making Bill feel better. Enjoy the snow globe effect through your window. Praying for you both.*
>
> *—Julie S*

> *Praise God! It is so great to hear that he has been able to sleep well. Our family is praying that you will feel God's unconditional love and comfort always. Thank you for the update. Lots of love.*
>
> *—Lisa D*

Post-chemo Day 4: Yuck

December 16, 2017

The two week window: chemo, the days after, and the brief days of rally before heading back into the gloom. Time becomes a crazy mix of friend and foe. Today has been so hard for Bill. He's discouraged and worried that we are barely to the halfway point and haven't started radiation and it's already kicking his strength right down the road like an old tin can. So many are rooting for him. Prayers are raining down on us and we feel it intensely. Yet, I am afraid. Hope feels far away and darkness is not my friend. This is the challenge tonight: find peace and trust in God. Dear friends, please pray for us. Thank you.

> *Hang in there.*
> *My prayer for the two of you: I need your help, dear God.*
> *Strengthen Marcia and Bill with Your love and your grace.*
> *Console them with your blessed Presence and grant the courage to persevere.*
> *—Nancy M*

> *You hem me in—behind and before; you have laid your hand upon me. Such knowledge is too wonderful for me, too lofty for me to attain.* **Psalm 139:5-6 (NIV)** *Thoughts and prayers for both of you.*
> *-Luana*

> *So very tough for you both right now.*
> *May you feel God's presence and may it give you comfort and strength.*
> *—Julie S*

> *I pray for uninterrupted sleep for both of you. Sleep "that knits up the raveled sleeve of care" (Shakespeare).*
> *—Linda and Jim*

> *Prayers are continuing for both of you. God works in ways that we don't understand at the time but he is always with you. I truly know what you are going through and it's rough, but please don't give up. You have many family and friends that care so much for both of you. Hugs and take care.*
> *—Cherryl*

> *Continued prayers for both of you. There really is a Bible verse that says God's got your back.* **Isaiah 58:8(NLT)** *says, "Your godliness will lead you forward, and the glory of the Lord will protect you from behind."*
> *—Sue*

Blessed

December 17, 2017

Thank you, friends and loved ones. The kind and supportive responses to yesterday's journal touched me deeply. If there is anything to be learned from this journey, it is knowing that when we feel weak or scared, there are those who listen. A caregiver feels so helpless. Last night was one of those times (and there will probably be many more) but I'm grateful for the wisdom. The reassurance. The advice was what I needed to get through this day. Thank you and God bless.

> *We are always here for you—but you know that! Love, hugs and prayers to you both.*
>
> *—Cindy M*

> *My husband Perry used to say that he thought it was harder to be the caregiver. Take care of yourself, Marcia, and remember prayers are for both of you.*
>
> *—Barbara*

> *Prayers continuing from us. Glad they help! Be sure to take care of yourself, too. It'll be best for both of you.*
>
> *—Cheryll*

> *Please know that you don't travel this journey alone. We are all here thinking of you both, keeping you close in thought and prayer and always wishing we could do something to help. Hoping Christmas time will be in Bill's favor for some good days and you're able to enjoy time with family. God Bless.*
>
> *—Karen P*

We Need a Little Christmas

December 18, 2017

Tonight carolers from church visited us. It was magical with the sound of Christmas carols lifting in the night. Standing at the front door with our arms around each other, we felt the promise of this season and love and warmth through the music. It was a peaceful moment and one we will cherish. Thank you, dear carolers, for making our home one of your stops.

> *You are seeing and appreciating the beauty and love that surrounds us. Thank you for the reminder. Have a lovely evening.*
>
> *—Diane*

> *The power of music and fellowship. lovely!*
>
> *—Julie S*

> *Love and steady prayers for both of you, and for all those caring for you, loving you, and supporting you. May the God of all being be with you on your way. And may many miracles of Christmas be yours. Take care.*
>
> *—Pat S*

Glorious Words

December 20, 2017

"I feel really good this morning!" Bill said as he sipped his coffee. Coffee! It tastes great today and it's been close to a month since he's been able to enjoy it. It is day nine after chemo and he's turned that corner and we also think one of his medications contributed to some of the pervasive malaise. If this holds, it's a real "ah-ha." Simply said, it's a beautiful day in the neighborhood, Mr. Rogers! Thanking God from whom all blessings flow.

> *Coffee! The greatest comfort food! So happy to hear Bill is enjoying a bit of "normal". May God continue to bless him!*
> *—Claudia*

> *Oh happy day!!*
> *—Margaret*

> *Oh, joy!*
> *—Sally*

> *One thing cancer does is teach us to appreciate the good things even more! Who knew a cup of coffee could bring such joy? Continue feeling better, Bill.*
> *—Barbara*

Word of the Day: Shrinking!

December 21, 2017

We met with a radiologist in Farmington today. He talked with Bill's oncologist so they are on the same page. Both of the doctors are waiting for direction from Dr. Evans, the surgeon, in Milwaukee. Treatment can go several ways: chemo with radiation, or chemo, surgery, and then radiation. It is up to Dr. Evans and we will know his recommendations January 8th. The radiologist wanted to know what symptoms Bill had initially and Bill told him he'd had lots of abdominal pain. The radiologist asked how the pain is now and Bill said "gone" which put a grin on the radiologist's face to which he responded, "Then the tumor is shrinking." *Lovely words* to us today!

> *That is wonderful news! Praying for continued blessings!*
> *—Claudia*

> *What a great Christmas present!*
> *—Barbara*

> *What wonderful news! Your posts mean so much. We share both the highs and lows. We are smiling and praising God today.*
> *—Linda S*

Zac and Bill who is modeling his Lions gear

Merry Christmas!

December 25, 2017

It's been a whirlwind of family coming and going but oh, what joy! All of our kids spent some part of the holiday with us which is rare as busy as they all are, and it was wonderful. We shared lots of laughter, fellowship, and food. Bill has been awfully tired, dizzy, and not feeling great but was a trouper and joined us for a few meals and socializing. Tomorrow is Chemo #4 and we hope the doctor will administer a dose of hydration fluids. It may delay chemo for a day or more but he may need a tune up before proceeding. As we end the day, it's our prayer that tomorrow will give him the "tweaks" he needs.

> *That would be the greatest gift after having those near and dear under one roof at the same time. Positive thoughts will be shadowing you tomorrow as you check back in. Careful on those roads, they are wicked to say the least. Many thanks for the regular updates.*
>
> *—Louann*

> *And the rollercoaster ride continues. So happy family was with you. Continued prayers.*
>
> *—Ginny*

> *I'm glad Christmas was a fun time. Prayers that this next chemo can somehow be made easier*
>
> *—Sue*

The Difference a Day Makes

December 26, 2017

Chemo went really well for Bill today! Maybe that's a bit of an oxymoron. Chemo and "well" in the same sentence. Bill saw the doctor and they started him off with fluids before chemo. It seems that was just what he needed because tonight he is pain/nausea/dizziness free. The doctor also mentioned that the bile duct that *was* blocked is now clear. What a Christmas gift! We know the treatment seems to be working. As Bill sleeps comfortably, I am rejoicing and thankful that today was truly a good day.

> *Marcia, this is such good news. We prayed for both of you at church during Sunday service and again at our candle light service Sunday night. May God continue to lay his hand on both of your shoulders and bring healing and peace! Please tell Bill hello.*
>
> *—Dianna*

> *We rejoice with you!*
>
> *—Sally P*

> *Your attitude of gratitude is in full gear today. I admire that about you two. You appreciate the small things. Sending smiles.*
>
> *—Linda & Jim*

> *Had a very close friend who went through pancreatic cancer and his mentor was wonderful interpreting, preparing for some outcomes, as well as moral support for all involved. I found him to be an incredible resource, too. Seems like there are good things in this cold air!*
>
> *-Louann*

Baby It's Cold Outside!

December 28, 2017

We're on our way to have Bill's chemo pump disconnected which feels so good to him when it is done. We will head home with a patch for 27 hours and *then*, it will be three weeks (instead of two) "off" from chemo— a welcome pause in the action. The cold wreaks havoc causing lots of neuropathy so I'll warm up the car and once we are home, he can stay put. Sending hugs of gratitude to all our prayer warriors and followers in this site.

> *Yay! A break will be very nice. Keep strong and look for a healthy future. You are both in my continued prayers.*
>
> *—Marla*

> *So glad you can stay put and look at the pretty snow from the warmth of inside!! Prayers continuing.*
>
> *—Cheryll*

> *Wow, that is terrific news! It is really cold out, make sure he bundles up. Would love to come and visit both of you. Praise to God, miracles happen! Have a Happy New Year. Prayers will keep coming.*
>
> *—Dianna*

Happy New Year

December 31, 2017

Today is our 21st wedding anniversary. We usually go out for an early dinner to avoid the late night party crowd, but this year stayed home to eat in our relatively germ free home. It's a funny New Year's Eve. Our resolution for 2018 isn't to lose weight or spend more time accomplishing projects. Our resolution is to stay positive, focus on God's plan, and find gratitude in every day. Bill felt relatively well today. He's awfully tired but good about sleeping when he needs it, and he was more like himself today. He bantered about the Lions football team and demonstrated more love and affection which are all things that are usually "normal." These days it can be too much. That's what I mean about gratitude. I don't need glitzy gifts. I am so grateful to see the man I love having a pretty good day. As the months progress there will be more challenges we know, but we look for that "light" at the end of the tunnel and keep moving in that direction. Peace, friends and loved ones, and happiest of New Years to you all.

Happy Anniversary Marcia and Bill. My hope is that 2018 will see a return of health for Bill. I pray for his doctors to have the knowledge needed to destroy the cancer and restore his health. Marcia, I also pray that God gives you the strength and courage you need to help Bill and be an advocate in his health care. May the New Year also be a new beginning of healing.

—Luana

Happy New Year, my friend. You have always had a positive outlook and a loving manner. You are the best person for Bill to have on his side.

—Marla

Happy "healing-versary". Sounds like a perfect day for you to be centered on one another and keep a positive, prayer filled attitude for 2018.

—Louann

Funny how life can suddenly show us its real priorities and values. Beautifully expressed, Marcia.

—Jim, Bill's brother-in-law

Happy Anniversary! And many more 'non-glitzy 'gifts like today!!

—Claudia

Helpful Interventions

January 4, 2018

There are a couple of new developments in this epic journey:

Beaumont and the medical staff/treatment is great, but the drive is brutal—especially when you feel crummy. Today Bill's Beaumont doctor wrote a standing order for supplemental fluids on non-chemo weeks at a cancer center in our hometown. So tomorrow morning, he will bundle up and get a dose of hydrating fluids a mere two miles from home. That is a big relief.

Secondly, Bill now has a mentor through a program the hospital offers. He's paired with someone who had the same diagnosis. Bill's mentor is two years post-surgery and doing well. He talked to Bill from Florida where he was about to play golf. (Bill said he heard a little too much detail regarding some aspects of treatment and surgery. Ignorance sometimes *is* bliss!) It's encouraging, though, to see the potential for normalcy that lies ahead and this man will be another resource to him.

Good news about the local fluids. Sounds like it will be much less draining. Also good news about the mentor. Only someone who's been there can truly understand. We heard from the cousin with pancreatic cancer I told you about today. She's still doing well and says she knows God has a plan for her so she tries to enjoy every day.

—Sue

What a blessing! This cold weather makes travel a challenge, but having to travel so close to home is definitely a boon.

—Linda S

Two pieces of good news-terrific! Less driving in January must give you enormous relief. The mentor is great news, too. Talking with someone who has truly walked the same path is priceless. May these positive events give you lots of comfort. Stay warm and take care of each other. We so appreciate these posts and prayer for you every day.

—Julie S

Poised and Ready

January 7, 2018

We're on our way to Milwaukee by way of Chicago. We enjoyed dinner and fellowship at the loving home of my sister Linda and her husband, Steve, niece Mackenzie, and our dear son, Zac. We so appreciate the love and support of these special people who help buoy us up when it's tough to feel cheery. Tomorrow, there will be tests and on Tuesday the consult with the doctor for his opinion on Bill's progress. Fervent prayers and hopes for optimistic news!

Thinking of all and hoping good news awaits. Cold weather: just help with shrinkage.

—Luann

Bill's sister, Carolyn, and I share Bill and Marcia's hopes, fears and anxiety. We share our love and prayers, trusting in eventual healing and a continued fulfilling life.

—Jim, Bill's brother-in-law

Prayers for safe travels, wise counsel, and positive news. Prayers of gratitude for your loving, supportive family. God bless.

—Julie S

"He will cover you with his feathers, and under his wings you will find refuge; his faithfulness will be your shield and rampart". **Psalm 91:4. (NIV)** *May each day bring you renewed strength and brighter times. Be very careful on the roads.*

—Dianna

Hope

January 9, 2018

There is a glorious sunrise out the expansive windows in the lab as we wait this morning. It affirms this is a day of hope and promise. As soon as we meet with the doctor, we'll share what I pray will be encouraging news.

Prayers continue for you and Bill. Positive thoughts for you both. God Bless!
—Julie S

Love, love, love your attitude. Prayers continue!
—Sally P

Sending positive thoughts and, since you are in my home state. Good things happen when you are in God's country!
—Louann

"Mid Term Grades"

January 9, 2018

Bill is half way through chemo. There are four more sets of infusions over the next two months.

He will start radiation two weeks after chemo finishes. The schedule will be chemo once a week for six weeks and radiation daily for the same amount of time. We've decided we will move to Milwaukee for the duration of the radiation. Two cancer markers have decreased by 50-67%; overall blood work is good, and the tumor has shrunk by one full centimeter.

It was an exhausting day with lots of information about next steps and the *huge* surgery to come, but for now—this moment— we're grateful for this "progress report". A glass of wine and a toast to the love of my life seems a perfect way to wrap up this important day.

> *Three cheers for joy and hope! And loads of "thank you" prayers. Steady prayers continue.*
> *—Pat S*

> *We will drink a toast to the two of you tonight, too. This is so encouraging. We are waging a battle together and we believe we will win. We know that a part of winning is our faithful and believing prayers in the Great Physician. Another part is the love we share. I picture David and Goliath. We are David.*
> *—Linda S*

> *You two were in my thoughts all day. Breathe! We continue prayers of strength, courage and healing from the great physician and his earthly helpers.*
> *—Nancy M*

> *This is the best possible news. We are all in this together and will keep the faith and prayers coming your way!*
> *—Louann*

> *So glad that you got some encouraging news. Prayers continue!*
> *—Cheryll*

> *It sounds like much of the news is promising. Fighting cancer seems much like fighting a war. It sounds like you are very wise taking each day one at a time. Prayers always!*
> *—Sue*

A New Plan

January 12, 2018

All the driving and coordinating between Michigan and Wisconsin doctors is becoming a bit overwhelming, so we've decided to move to Milwaukee very soon and stay until Bill recovers from surgery and can travel home. We're hunting online for a place to rent (hopefully furnished) and making the move sooner than later. The downside is that we will be isolated from our community and those who are so caring— but we have our Chicago clan about 90 minutes away which will be a big help. So, please pray for a quick housing solution, dear friends and family, so we can move forward in this journey toward restored health. Updates to follow as they come.

> *I think it is a great idea. Cut down on the things you have control over to make this journey as easy as possible. Prayers and thoughts will follow you everywhere you go.*
>
> *—Louann*

> *We are all going with you -maybe not physically-but mentally and spiritually and lovingly. You will never walk alone.*
>
> *—Linda S*

> *You do what is best. Continued prayers on this journey. Thanks so much for taking time to keep us updated.*
>
> *—Ginny*

Chemo #5

January 16, 2018

Bill got his diagnosis three months ago today and three weeks after that the doctor told him he could expect to live six months without treatment and twelve to fifteen months with it. After that he sought a second opinion and how glad we are that we did because now he is on a course to be cured! Thank you, God!

When Bill saw his oncologist today at Beaumont he told him he feels great. That really pleased him and he responded with, "That's great! High five!" The oncologist and surgeon in Milwaukee had a conference call after which Bill's oncologist told us that he "gushed" about how good his pancreas looks! Now that might be a peculiar thing to gush about, but in our world these days, that's terrific news—translation: on a course for surgery!

Tomorrow Bill will have extra hydration to keep his body happy. Thursday, after the chemo pump is removed, we will head home. It's been relatively serene day with definite good news.

> A strong will, determination, love, support, and prayer are surely paying off. How great to read this!
>
> —Louann

> Wonderful news! Serene days mean everything!
>
> —Sue

> Happiness is a "gushing" doctor and a good looking pancreas. Blessings are coming your way. Praise God!
>
> —Sally P

> Glad to hear your praise report! Thank you, Jesus, for your continued blessings and healing.
>
> —Cindy H

> Reading this post was a wonderful way to begin my day! Continuing to keep you both in our prayers!
>
> —Nancy B

> So happy to have such good news and better days!
>
> —Linda, Marcia's sister

> Wonderful! Keep the great news rolling in. "Nice pancreas!" Bet no one has said that to you before!
>
> —Nancy H

The Aftermath

January 20, 2018

As chemo treatments progress, patients typically feel worse but Bill seems to be managing the side effects and symptoms pretty well. He's very weary and feels weak, but some of the "uglier" symptoms are effectively managed by the doctors. It's amazing to see how they can tweak subtle combinations of drugs to ease the effect on a patient and still maintain a course of eventual healing. That's the news from the Wright abode this morning.

> *Thanks for the update. Enjoy this beauty of a day!*
> *—Cindy M*

> *Blessings to all who are caring for Bill. His strength, both physically and spiritually, depend on the love and prayers. Thanks to all you wonderful partners in this struggle.*
> *—Carolyn and Jim, Bill's sister and brother-in-law*

> *Good news, Marcia. Glad you are both able to be home for a bit. Take care. You both continue to be in our thoughts and prayers. God Bless.*
> *—Julie S*

House Hunting

January 23, 2018

Bill will get a dose of hydration here in town tomorrow and Thursday we go to Milwaukee to apartment hunt. We have seven places to check out and are hoping one will be just right. We will move at the very end of February and start chemo and radiation there in early March. During this visit we're meeting another Michigan couple whose story is very similar. They live there now and will have the surgery in two weeks. It will be great to be able to talk and share experiences. Please pray we find a place to call "home" for these vital months.

> *I just know this will be a time when things come together. Even knowing the other couple will be such a benefit as you all know the trials, fears, hopes, etc. connected with this. Get ready for some good beer and cheese curds from my home state!*
>
> *—Louann*

> *Prayers that the right apartment will be found where you can rest and be comfortable and that the other couple can give you some insights and support.*
>
> *—Sue*

> *Prayers you want? Prayers you got!*
>
> *—Linda S*

New Digs

January 26, 2018

Our new temporary home is a brand new apartment on the fourth floor with an elevator. It's fresh and bright with eastern exposure windows that let in lots of morning sun. When the weather breaks there is a balcony where we can enjoy the fresh air. It's an important backdrop for what lies ahead. Establishing a serene and calm environment where Bill can relax, recover, and heal is the priority in our new "home".

We met the delightful Michigan couple who are also going through the pancreatic cancer journey. It was so meaningful to talk with these people. This man will have his surgery in two weeks— so he is "ahead" of Bill. We forged a unique friendship in just a few hours but we left feeling infinitely connected. Tomorrow we head home and get ready for chemo.

Another answered prayer. Praise God. I can just visualize your new place.
—Linda S

Mission accomplished! What a special connection, too, with others on the same journey. Safe travels!
—Julie S

So glad that you have found a tranquil haven in the midst of all of this upheaval. Prayers for similar successes in the future. One step at a time.
—Cheryll

Oh joy! The plan is unfolding so beautifully! New condo and new friends! Love to you both.
—Sally P

I'm so glad you found something that will work nicely. I'm also glad that you were able to connect with the other couple. Nobody can understand what you are going through unless they've been there, too. Prayers that chemo goes well this time.
—Sue

75%

January 30, 2018

When you're married to a man who loves numbers, ¾ of the way through chemo is an accomplished hurdle. We will move to Milwaukee March 1ˢᵗ where Bill will begin radiation with supplemental chemo for six weeks. It's a daunting physical challenge but he is so tough and strong. I deeply admire his determination. Tonight he is resting but feeling pretty good. As much as there is ahead of him (and us), we are in a good place tonight. We said how lucky we are to be together, to love each other, and have so many dear people who pray for us and wish us well.

Having each other is a huge blessing! Keeping you both in our prayers!
—Claudia

Making it through 75% is a really big deal! Congratulations to both of you and prayers for the next 25%.
—Sue

You are both amazing in this struggle. In terms of the numbers guy, I estimate 110%. Hats off to you both.
—Louann

I share all your updates with my dear husband Jim. You two have confirmed what we have come to know over the years: together, we make each other stronger. Our prayers and love continue, dear ones.
—Linda S

You both are in our prayers
—Dody

Prayers continue for each of you! 100%!
—Nancy H

Marcia and her sister Linda toast to a good day's work

We're In!

February 9, 2018

Since our lease begins February 1st (we are obligated to a minimum of six months) we did some preliminary moving over the week end. With the amazing help of my son Zac, we took two very full vehicles to Wisconsin. My sister, Linda, met us there and we unloaded everything into carts and moved them into the apartment. 24 hours later we had furniture assembled and things put away. We shopped for food, miscellaneous household items, and a TV. Blow up mattresses made beds for us all the first night. The only glitch in all of the logistics came when we discovered our new bed was not going to be delivered as scheduled. At this writing we are still resolving this mix-up but *hopefully* will have a real bed in a day or two. Bill has chemo at home on Tuesday and we're back here in three weeks for the duration. Weather reports tell us there is a big snowstorm at home and snow is really coming down here, too, but we're coping pretty well.

I can just see you all bustling about bringing order out of chaos. You will make it a lovely home because you have that gift. And the drawers will all be organized before you move in. I am sure of it!

—Linda S

Wow!! It made me tired just reading what you did!! What a nice condo you have. Have a safe trip home. Take care.

—Cherryl

Herculean effort. Well done. Glad for this cozy nest for you through the Milwaukee stay. Thankful for your safe travels. Put your feet up, rest. God bless.

—Julie S

You all are amazing! I think you are filled with the Spirit. The love of your family just shines through. And yes, Linda S is right- your apartment will be a beautiful home and the spices will be in alphabetical order.

—Diane

I am also amazed at all that you all got done. (Not surprised as I know you, Marcia!) It already looks like home. Best wishes and prayers are sent to all of you wherever you are on this journey.

—Louann

On Its Way

February 11, 2018

Settling our Wisconsin digs has gone smoothly— except for the bed. Wouldn't you think this is mighty important for someone who needs lots of rest? After several phone calls and panicked requests we discovered they accidentally dropped us from the schedule. But today is the day! We are staying an extra day for the delivery. Given the huge snowfall here and forecast at home for more, it's probably a good decision. God looks out for us even when we don't think so.

Our new friends from Michigan called to let us know his surgery was a success. We may be able to see him today for a very brief visit which is another silver lining to this hiccup in the move.

Great news!

—Louann

Staying put is a good option for everyone in this corner of the world. Rest as best you can. Hope that bed gets there STAT! Love & Prayers always.

—Julie S

So glad things are working out. Take care and prayers continue.

—Cherryl

Chemo #7

February 13, 2018

As chemotherapy drips into his body, Bill says he feels great this morning. With one more round to go, he's already researching the chemo that will be paired with radiation. He is a highly engaged participant in his treatment. As foreign as all this seemed at the beginning, it's now a macabre but familiar routine.

> *Funny how our perspective changes as life gives us its twists and turns. I think it will really help Bill to be proactive in his treatment.*
>
> —Luana

> *I am sitting here listening to Brahms, fire in the fireplace, warm and cozy, using this as a time of prayer for you and Bill. My heart is filled with love and faith that The Great Physician will guide the hands of all who treat Bill and that they will be at the top of their skills working together to follow with precision the course of treatment. I pray, knowing that your love for each other adds a healing of its own. I send you my love, dear ones.*
>
> —Linda & Jim

> *On this very special day of "love" know that back home we all love both of you and are keeping you both (including your children-young adults) in our prayers.*
>
> —Dianna

The Value of Love

February 14, 2018

On this "day of love", we send happy and loving wishes to all our followers. Thank you all for your love and support!

> *Happy Valentine's Day! Love you both.*
>
> *—Cindy H*

> *Love and prayers to both of you.*
>
> *—Ginny*

> *Happy Valentine's Day to you both. Prayers and good thoughts. God Bless!!!*
> *—Julie S*

> *Wishing you both a wonderful Valentine's Day. Prayers are continuing for both of you.*
>
> *—Cherryl*

> *Happy Valentine's Day to both of you! Love is a powerful foe against sickness!*
>
> *—Sue*

There's No Place Like Home

February 15, 2018

We're home from a "chemo week" and will actually be here for eleven days before we have to pack a bag. Bill is resting and tolerating this round well. Tired, a bit wobbly on his feet, experiencing quirky reactions to cold liquids, but relatively content. There is chicken pot pie for dinner (thanks, Costco!) and it's a good night to snuggle in and watch the Olympics by the fire. For our non-local followers it's really foggy today!

> *So glad you are both able to be home for a bit. Enjoy your snuggle time watching the Olympics.*
> *—Julie S*

> *Enjoy your evening snuggled in!*
> *—Claudia*

> *Eleven days..... enjoy that respite. Moving forward, moving forward-.love and prayers to you both.*
> *—Louann*

"Chemocation"

My friend, Gretchen, shared this funny phrase meaning a break from chemo treatments. It's so nice to do ordinary things: have lunch with former work friends, run non-medical errands, and go to the local symphony concert. That's what we can't lose sight of: life continues on and we must stay with it as time passes. Becoming lost in cancer isn't good for anyone— even though it's hard not to be. Bill says "I'd like a day without (thinking about or tending to) cancer." That's fair, I'd say!

Love that term...and glad you are on one for right now! Enjoy the music tonight, friends.

—Louann

Enjoy. Glad you are having some fun. Although, knowing the two of you, I suspect you have some fun every day.
I found a handmade valentine this week given to me by a third grade student years ago. Red construction paper, a doily, lots of tape and a hand written note that said, "You are the beast teacher I every had." Considering that student, it was the beast valentine I ever got from a student. True story.

—Linda & Jim

"Weighting"

February 20, 2018

Now that the momentum is set, these last few days at home make us restless. Bill has his last three days of chemo at Beaumont next week and then we move. We're watching how well he tolerates this final round. Right now he feels weaker, more fatigued, and had some black outs even though he's getting extra hydration. The buildup in his system is cumulative and creates variables we can't predict. The next leg of the journey is fraught with unknowns. Will the new scans show more shrinkage? Will radiation be tolerable? What will cardiology say about the wear and tear of chemo on the heart? (Oh yeah, the stent from last May with its many complications). Then, after all this, is the surgery scheduled. Once they explore laparoscopically, they have to rule out any potential spread...but that happens on the day of the *big* surgery.

Providing all is clear, they will proceed with a surgery that will exceed eight hours. The doctor will remove the tumor and reconstruct new vasculature with a jugular vein and another from the thigh.

Wow. It seems daunting, immense, and terrifying all in one package called "curing cancer". There are so many "ifs," so many hurdles to get past, and it could be for naught. It could be there is more cancer. Maybe they won't be able to operate—and then we are out of options. We've based all of these decisions *hoping* and *believing* this will work. The cold, hard reality is that it *might* not. That weighs heavily right now on this rainy, gloomy day. We just don't know.

Prayer has been a comfort and the verbal support of so many encouraging friends and family. But today there is no comfort. Today there is just the "weight."

> *Marcia, you put to words so eloquently the fears you, Bill, and all who love you struggle to keep down. Sometimes it can help. I believe you are people of faith and we are invited to lay our burdens at the feet of our Lord. I pray that you can find even a few minutes relief from your "weight". We get through the tough times minute by minute and day by day. God bless!*
> *—Claudia*

I say you are in the midst of many miracles starting with the idea that there were few, if any options at the start. The odds may be long but are way shorter than when you began this uninvited trip. I say, all of us just need to know that there are those who survive and you have met some, as I have. I am assuming that Bill is in that elite group and will one day be sharing his story, as will you, with those who are just starting out. I have only positive thoughts about the outcome and that is where our minds need to go, and will, with prayer and the kinship you two have with so many. Hang tough friends. Easy to say and hard to do but it is our only choice in my view.

—Louann

Our hearts are heavy, too. We are left to strip away what we know doesn't work or help: worry, fear, and doubts; and embrace what we know can and does work and help: faith, prayer and love. Our Lord and God even gives us the faith we sometimes lack and the strength to look ahead with hope. Thank you, dear friend, for sharing the good, the bad and the ugly of this remarkable journey. We are here to go the next step with you.

—Linda S

Such a difficult journey you are both taking. I read this prayer today that seems to have been written for you. "God of surprising journeys, help me to live my life forward, trusting that you are steering the ship. Help me to understand my life backward by seeing and forgiving the many signs of Jonah." Right now you are truly in the belly of the whale. Praying for new life beyond this trial and the strength to move through it

—Diane

Taking Action!

February 24, 2018

A great day! Bill felt good: "normal!" he said.

We've tackled the last of the preparations before the "move". The taxes are at the CPA's office, yard maintenance is set for our time of absence, and we went to a matinee movie. It felt like a pretty typical Saturday and then—wait for it: Bill decided to get some time in on his elliptical! So proud of his tenacity and feeling so much more hopeful.

> *Wow! I'm so happy to hear this! This is the best news ever!*
>
> *—Shannon*

> *What a wonderful day. Bless you both.*
>
> *—Margaret*

> *I wish you both many, many more days of "normal".*
>
> *—Sue*

> *Such a fantastic day for both of you. Continued good thoughts and prayers for your journey.*
>
> *—Julie S*

> *So glad to hear you had a "normal" day. Prayers continuing.*
>
> *—Cherryl*

> *Good to hear that things are progressing. Sounds like a good day for you both. Hope for more to come.*
>
> *—Ginny*

A "Value Added" Plan

February 26, 2018

Some excitement: Bill's son, Aaron, is moving to Milwaukee for six months. The firm he works for has asked him to work in the Milwaukee office for this period of time which means Aaron will be nearby while we are there. To be sure, the hand of God is on this one! My son Zac is in Chicago and my sister Linda and family are in the suburbs of the city. We thought having them an hour and a half away was great (and it truly is) but this is turning into a viable family reunion.

> *God's way of moving love and support even closer. WOW! Our God is a mighty God. Hallelujah!*
>
> —*Linda S*

> *I have loved catching up on this journal and seeing how God has been involved each step of the way! Much love to you as your family continues down this road.*
>
> —*Stephanie*

> *Sometimes things are just "supposed to be." What blessings! Who'd have guessed they'd be in Milwaukee? Might turn all of you into Milwaukee football, baseball, and basketball fans :-)*
> *Continued love and prayers.*
>
> —*Pat*

> *How exciting for you and Bill. There is nothing like having family close. God works in mysterious ways.*
>
> —*Julie S*

> *If I believed in coincidences I would think this was an amazing one. God's hand is in this.*
>
> —*Diane*

> *I'm so happy that this is all falling into place for you! Family support is going to be crucial and so much nicer if it doesn't have to be from far away. "No one fights alone" is such a good slogan to remember.*
>
> —*Sue*

Eight is Enough

February 27, 2018

Last day for chemo!

We are at Beaumont and Bill was the first patient in the chemo room to be "hooked up" so he will finish earlier than usual. He's in his favorite recliner (the one with most space around it) and is enjoying a fly tying magazine from his friend, Sherm. Now he's dreaming of fishing for pike! This treatment may not be something you look forward to, but knowing this is "it" lifts his spirits and he's relaxed. We're off to a reasonably good day.

> *Those pike are cruising in Portage Lake not far from your sister's home. Remember there is good lodging and food with a family guide. We look forward to it.*
> *—Jim, Bill's brother-in-law*

> *Nice of you to let Bill read that magazine first, Marcia! Ha ha. May the rest of this big week go smoothly. Traveling mercies.*
> *—Julie S*

> *Your "lucky cricket" is feeling happy for you!*
> *—Linda, Marcia's sister*

> *This is quite an accomplishment to have this part behind you. Prayers that this chemo is well tolerated and safe travels for you this week. Those pike are going to be fished out of the water before they know it!*
> *—Sue*

> *Good news! Hope things continue to go well.*
> *—Ginny*

Fatigue Settles In

February 28, 2018

The aftermath of chemo varies but this round has produced a very tired man. Bill slept lots yesterday and now he is getting an infusion that helps with hydration. Once finished, we will go back to the hotel for a nap. This isn't terribly exciting but it's so important to allow the chemo drugs to work and lead his body toward healing. I'm finding it's a great opportunity to practice walking in the mall across the street.

This is a sacrifice.

Well, OK. Not really.

> Get yourself a little iPod and load up some awesome Christian music...and then "walk on sister"! :) Glad he is getting some rest. Remember to provide that for his wife too! Hugs.
>
> —Sally R

> At least the mall is a change of scenery. Good to know he is resting and hope you get some too.
>
> —Ginny

> Buy some new shoes!
>
> —Marla

> Malls are good medicine too! Prayers for both of you continue.
>
> —Cherryl

> You have such a good attitude! I love walking the malls. When my daughter, Kylee was small and in kindergarten, I would walk the malls holding little Ryan waiting until school was out for the day. My goal was not to be passed by a couple of 80 year olds. They passed me for years!
>
> —Lisa D

Jenn and Bill the day before we left for Wisconsin

Moving Eve

March 1, 2018

Tomorrow is the day we move to Wisconsin. When it came right down to it, the piles we're loading into the car seemed too big tonight so we opted to get a good night's rest and tackle it fresh in the morning. My daughter Jenn joined us for dinner and a visit. Good friends and ultra-special neighbors, Bob and Cindy brought travel goodies and good wishes so we just decided to enjoy that-and call it a night. We know we won't have these moments for quite a while and they are so special. So, packing- you have to wait. We made some good memories tonight!

> *Perfect plan and great night to be in, given the "Snowmagedon" we are experiencing. Great to have these memories to pack as they take no room and will provide as much, or more, than the things you will be packing! My home state of Wisconsin cannot wait to have you, in spite of the reason. We are always looking for more cheese heads!*
>
> *—Louann*

> *Sending love, hugs and prayers to you and safe travels as you start this next chapter...we are cheering you both on! Make it a great day!*
>
> *—Cindy H*

> *Great decision-packing a few memories before heading out. The sun is shining on your travel day. May all go smoothly.*
>
> *—Julie S*

This is It!

March 2, 2018

It's a gorgeous sunny morning and in spite of the heavy snow yesterday, the roads are dry for travel to Milwaukee. Oddly I'm feeling emotional this morning. I stayed home to "clean our way out the door" while Bill has an infusion here in town. The house is too quiet. As I converse with God, I thank Him for all He's provided to us so far: good friends and caring people, terrific medical resources, and His abiding love. Yet there is the vulnerability to this "mission" and I ask for your prayers, dear ones, to give me the strength to support the man I love so much. Thank you all.

Jesus, invade Marcia and Bill's day. Bring the peace that only You can provide! Hold her heart right now. Allow her to rest in Your grace and unending love. You are so crazy, madly in love with Bill and Marcia. Let them feel it today! We trust Your word and Your promises that never come back void. Raise them up Lord! Because of who You are! Amen.

—*Sally R*

Dear Lord Jesus, when you walked upon this earth, You healed the sick, gave sight to the blind, caused the lame to walk, and raised the dead. Now I come to You on behalf of Bill who is suffering today and pray that You would send Bill and Marcia your healing power. You yourself have suffered all things. You know and understand their pain. I ask you to ease their suffering, to quiet their fears, and to direct their eyes to Your cross. Teach them to place themselves into Your gracious care, saying, "Not my will but Yours be done." Hear my prayer for Your name's sake. May God bless your families always in all things. Amen.

—*Dianna*

May the road rise to meet you -
May the wind be always at your back
The sun shine warm upon your face
The rain fall soft upon your fields
And until we meet again may God hold you (and Bill) in the palm of his hand.

—*Luana*

*Prayers **every** day, Marcia! For as long as you need them!*
—Linda L

Have a safe trip and prayers are continuing for both you and Bill.
— Cherryl

Prayers for both of you! It must be terribly hard leaving home to go into the unknown.
—Sue

A New Home Sweet Home!

March 2, 2018

We're here! The place is unpacked and settled and it feels really good. Aaron is with us tonight— an extra nice perk. A local restaurant had a great fish fry so we enjoyed a takeout and relaxed. It was perfect.

We're grateful to all of you readers for your prayers and kind words. The drive went without incident and we unloaded everything we needed. Whew!

The rest of the week end is getting acclimated to the routines- grocery shopping, etc. And my Chicago sister and her husband are coming for an overnight on Sunday to help us celebrate Bill's birthday which is Monday. The time with those we love is the best.

> *Glad you made it safely......... Life is good.*
> *—Cindy*

> *Glad to hear you made it safely. Enjoy your birthday, Bill. Take care.*
> *—Cherryl*

> *I'm so glad you got there safely and are starting to settle in!*
> *—Sue*

> *I can almost hear a little "calm" in your voice of finally being "home". Remember that anywhere you are with Bill can be considered "home", and I have no doubt that you will do all the necessary "touches" to make it very cozy for the both of you! Happy Birthday Bill! May God give you extra special favor and honor rewards today! Love and hugs.*
> *—Sally P*

> *Happy Birthday, Bill! Glad you made it to where you need to be to deal with current challenges. Thoughts and prayers will continue from the Spaulding family*
> *—Keith*

The birthday boy and his cake

Happy Birthday?

March 5, 2018

Today is Bill's birthday. Family from Chicago drove up yesterday to celebrate with us. We had dinner at a nearby restaurant with ice cream and cake at "home". He's smiling but is very, very tired. Today, his actual birthday was somewhat marred because he had to fast for tests at the hospital. By the time we got home, he was ravenous, ate very little, and went to bed. Tomorrow we meet with both the radiation oncologist and surgeon and pray we'll have some encouraging news. This birthday boy really needs some optimism in his reports.

> *Prayers that you and Bill both get a good night's rest and that the news from the tests will be good!*
>
> *—Sue*

> *We wish both of you courage, fortitude and healing in the year ahead. Continued prayers.*
>
> *—Nancy M*

> *Happy Birthday, Bill. Looking good in the picture! Keeping you and Marcia in our prayers.*
>
> *—Ginny*

> *Bill, hope you had a great birthday and get some positive news tomorrow. I will be praying tonight for a good report. Thanks and God bless both of you.*
>
> *—Dianna*

> *What an awesome cake! Too cute! Yesterday we celebrated with you both for Bill's birthday. Today we go with you in spirit for all your testing. And then tomorrow we already claim the good news! Your faithfulness is a testimony to us all. Lean into what I read this morning:*
> *"Come to Me, all ye that labor and I will give you rest. Take My yoke upon you and learn of Me, for I am meek and lowly in heart, and you will find rest unto your souls. For My yoke is easy and My burden is light."* **Matthew 11:28-30 (KJVA)**
>
> *—Sally R*

Let's hope Bill gets a wonderful birthday present.

—Barbara

Happy Birthday Bill! Your cake looks awesome! Hoping tomorrow is great birthday news!

—Marla

A State of Inertia

March 6, 2018

Today we learned the tumor has not changed in size and the cancer markers are up. We feel discouraged and anxious. The radiation oncologist met with us for a long time and she is prepared to move forward with radiation and chemo based on Dr. Evans' recommendation. Dr. Evans stated radiation *is* the next step, so that is in motion. We meet tomorrow with a radiation team to "plan". This will take about ten days to prepare. Treatment will last five and a half weeks with chemo once a week during that time. The goal will be to shrink the tumor and pulverize any sneaky cells that are undesirable (my interpretation). After this course of treatment, he must wait a month, have another scan, and if all is clear, the surgery will happen. The surgery Dr. Evans described will be very difficult— the most complicated he has performed.

Bill meets with cardiology tomorrow to make sure everything is being managed appropriately with respect to his heart. So while we aren't "flying high," we are glad to be "moving forward." It looks like after tomorrow we will have some days to enjoy the area and maybe do a little sightseeing.

Not what you wanted to hear, but our time is not His time.
So, time to regroup, round up more prayer warriors, and get to work! Time to fight! I'm in!

—Sally R

Prayers that things will become better than they seem at this moment. Enjoy the few days of respite before more treatments!

—Sue

Life is a rollercoaster, as you're experiencing. Keep the faith and we'll continue the prayers for good news.

—Ginny

Thinking of you guys. Hoping the next scan will show good progress. Sending lots of positive thoughts!

—Nancy H

The Early Bird Gets the Worm

March 7, 2018

It's 6:00 AM and we're back at the Cancer Center for labs and the preparation for radiation. It will be a long day since Bill's infusion isn't until 3:30. I'm already panicking about meal prep! There's no time for the simplest routines. Hopefully it will get better.

> *Big hugs to you both from home. Prayers for a smooth day filled with skilled care and good counsel.*
>
> *—Julie*

> *Yes, the day will be long and tiring. Funny how sitting and waiting is so tiring. As far as prepping dinner - maybe this will be a night for take-out/delivery. Saying prayers not only for you and Bill— but for the doctors and nurses who will be making critical decisions about Bill's care.*
>
> *—Luana*

> *Your life is not your own when dealing with cancer. You just have to say it is what it is and go with the flow. Easier said than done, I know. Sometimes you can't even go a day at a time but cut it into shorter chunks. Walk around the hospital. Find the gift shop. Get acquainted with the cafeteria. Go sit in the chapel. You know many prayers are coming your way. Take care.*
>
> *—Barbara*

> *You and Bill are daily in my prayers. It is mentally exhausting - just waiting. You have so many family and friends who care for both of you so much. The Lord has a plan. Take care and prayers are continuing.*
>
> *—Cherryl*

> *God Bless You and Bill during these long days. Hugs, love, blessings and prayers.*
>
> *—Lisa D*

> *Bless your hearts. You are now in your "apartment sweet apartment"... hopefully your haven to rest and comfort each other.*
>
> *—Carolyn and Jim, Bill's sister and brother-in-law*

The Day Got Better

March 7, 2018 continued

After my fretful rant in this morning's journal update, I gathered my wits and took heed from the wise postings of friends and loved ones.

Between Bill's appointments and an infusion we went home and slept for two hours! It was *so* helpful. Then back at the infusion center the nurse was a sweetheart. She was caring and bubbly. It gave us a big lift to talk about ordinary topics and not cancer. She shared a popular local spot for pizza so we took salad and pizza home. Heavenly!

After a hot shower I felt totally refreshed. Bill is resting very comfortably tonight and Aaron is with us so there is great contentment right now.

The schedule for Bill is unfolding as follows:

Radiation starts Monday, March 19 for five and a half weeks
Radiation: Monday through Friday
Chemo: Tuesdays
Infusion/hydration: Monday, Wednesday, Friday
And on the weekends? Rest.

Okay prayer warriors........ here is OUR schedule:

Radiation days*: PRAY Chemo day: PRAY*
Infusion/hydration days*: PRAY*
Bottom line*: we have one major way to impact the lives of both Bill and Marcia as they are walking through this season and that is through the mighty power of prayer! We serve a big God! A Mighty God! A God of miracles! So let's commit to letting Marcia and Bill know that we are praying daily for them and for God to invade their lives and remove this cancer! In the meantime, we ask that Bill and Marcia can be an amazing light to all those they come in contact with! Time for us all to put on His armor and win this battle—one day, one prayer at a time. Hugs.*
—Sally R

Pizza, shower, rest. Gratitude for simple pleasures. All good!
Know that we lift prayers for you daily. Strength and healing, strength and healing, strength and healing.

—Julie S

Our God is an AWESOME God!!! He is walking with you every step of the way on this journey. Prayers for you and Bill as well as for the wonderful doctors and helpful nurses that God is providing for you.

—Linda S

Time for a Weekend

March 9, 2018

The schedule is set for the coming weeks and today Bill had a fluid infusion. That's all. It was a simple day. Easy on his body. No extra tests or appointments. And tonight we again enjoyed a terrific fish take out from that popular restaurant. Aaron is with us. We watched movies and relaxed. In all, it was a normal night and boy, does that feel good! The week end is open with no medical tests or schedules until Monday. *How wonderful!*

> *Rest and normal are two really great words! Have a wonderful and relaxing weekend!*
>
> —Sue

> *So good to have this break and finding good food is a bonus. Enjoy the weekend.*
>
> —Louann

> *Have a wonderful and peaceful weekend. Nothing like takeout and enjoying family.*
>
> —Julie S

Taking Advantage of a Good Day

March 11, 2018

It's a beautiful day in Wisconsin so we visited the Mitchell Park Domes in Milwaukee. These enormous domes built in the 1960s have three different biomes: desert, tropical and a temperate "show" dome consisting of flowers, greenery, miniature trains, fantasy creatures, and animals. This last dome is very popular with families. It was relaxing and gorgeous. Afterwards, Bill, Aaron, and I drove along the Lake Michigan shoreline from the "other side." Tomorrow: infusions. But today was a good day to be normal.

> *Isn't it good to be "normal"? Missed you in choir this morning. (Light crowd - we sang the Irish Blessing). Thoughts and prayer always.*
>
> —*Luana*

> *"It is of the Lord's mercies that we are not consumed, because his compassions fail not. They are new every morning: great is thy faithfulness."* (**Lamentations 3:22-23**) *KJV Hold on to that! Grace and peace to you both.*
>
> —*Sally P*

Tests

March 13, 2018

We're back at the Cancer Center. Bill had hydration infusions yesterday and this morning they are checking the function of his kidneys. Radiation is hard on this organ and since he had radiation *many* years ago, the doctor wants to make sure he is safe for radiation next Monday. We continue to be impressed with the level of care along with the detailed diagnostic measures that continue to affirm our decision to be here. Reassurance is a comforting word on the cancer journey.

> *All sounds great and glad you are there on your temporary leave of absence from the Mitten State!*
>
> —*Louann*

> *Sounds like they're being careful in their decision making. Continuing prayers.*
>
> —*Ginny*

> *May God bless you both as you go through these difficult times ahead. Enjoy each good moment no matter how small. You are held in my prayers for healing, comfort, rest and peace.*
>
> —*Pam L*

You Get What You Pay For

March 15, 2018

Short term rental living and short term furnishings are sensible because they're affordable, but not necessarily comfy for the long haul. Bill's joints are complaining about the economy seating, so today we bit the bullet and bought an electronic lift chair for him. It's much more comfortable and moves into all kinds of positions. When Bill has his surgery, he will be able to use it to stand using the remote controls which will help with recovery. I'm hoping I'll get a chance to try out the fun controls, too. This could become our new hobby during the March Madness tournament.

> *Please don't hit the secret "eject" button on that chair. That would not be fun.*
>
> *—Linda S*

> *Just don't get the TV remote and the chair remote mixed up. Ha ha! Enjoy all the conveniences you can lay your hands on.*
>
> *—Margaret*

> *You are always thinking, and this chair purchase is a good thing! Don't know if it can make the NCAA games any better, but at least you will be comfortable. Games yesterday were super. Now, Go Green! Blessings.*
>
> *—Sally P*

Sweet 16 and Other Celebrations

March 18, 2018

It's been a weekend of basketball but no Irish whiskey. March Madness is a highlight at our house. We create brackets and enjoy the family competition. Zac is leading this year and I'm miraculously in second place. The new chair has not catapulted anyone onto the deck and Bill thinks it's much more comfortable. He is in a lot of pain, though, and we're not sure why. The usual measures aren't working so we have the option of going to the 24 hour Cancer Center or wait until tomorrow when he starts radiation and chemo— a very heavy day. I'm hoping Bill will be agreeable to a little drive to the Cancer Center when he gets up this morning. As miserable as he feels, sleep is not something I want to interrupt. So Prayer Warriors, please activate your healing thoughts and let our precious God know we're in need.

The Glen Ellyn "warriors" are on it...... and hoping today brings even a little relief to the pain.
—Linda, Marcia's sister

Yep, if he is still miserable a trip needs to happen. No need to suffer when there might be a solution. He needs all the energy to face tomorrow as do you. So the prayers and thoughts have been put on the super-fast track to you all.
—Louann

Praying for God's healing touch and that Marcia, Bill and the entire family feels His presence and love.
—Carolyn and Jim, Bill's sister and brother-in-law

Storming the heavens! Even through that disappointing Spartan loss :-(Strength, healing, love and peace to you all.
—Pat S

Our fervent prayer warriors have not stopped one single day for you both! Let me share these two scriptures that came across my journal this morning.... right after finishing prayer time-perfect to hang your hat on for today:

Hebrews 13:5 "Never will I leave you; never will I forsake you" (NIV)

Deuteronomy 31:8 "Do not be afraid (or discouraged) for it is the Lord who goes with you!"(AMP)

How awesome that we have a Father who always goes ahead to make sure things are as He intends! Keep the faith, as He is relying on you to be His ambassadors of ones praising Him in the storm!

And keep those brackets going as well! Go Blue!

—Sally R

And So It Begins

March 19, 2018

In yet another waiting room I wait. Today is Bill's first radiation treatment but no one can accompany him into the treatment area. I reflect. Today Bill said *again* "I'm going to beat this!" My heart jumped for joy because it's what we hope for—trusting in God's plan for him.

Yet it's still a teeny bit scary. It's a teeny bit unnerving. It's a lot of worry I must give to Him to carry for me. There is such challenge in this faith walk!

The encouragement, love, and prayers Caring Bridge© followers send are just the best.

When I am weak, you "give His angels charge over (me) thee"! **Psalm 91:11 KJV**

Thank you, Bridge readers and commentators! *You* are our angels. You bless us with care and love across the miles and "it is well with my soul."

> *The Lord loves you both so much and He is in charge of all that is going on. Prayers continue to comfort you and Bill as He guides you both through this challenge. Hugs!*
>
> *—Cherryl*

> *Just read what you have written over this unwelcome trip, Marcia. It is the Lord who has been there for both of you and your families to get you where you are. Without Bill's attitude and your support, there would be no hope. With this attitude there is nothing but hope and the best outcome. My two cents worth for today, kiddo.*
>
> *—Louann*

> *Marcia, you are so right to trust in the Lord. We are told to put these worries in his hands. Bless you and Bill both on this very hard journey. There are so many of your friends praying for a great outcome.*
>
> *—Julie S*

Okay so here you go:

Pray big prayers.............. and then expect what God can do!
I am not praying for some improvement, but full healing— not feeling a little better, but full healing! We serve a God of miracles. So many things we will simply not understand until we see Him face to face— so for now we pray bold prayers, and get out of His way and let Him show off in Bill! Such big hugs for you today, Marcia!

—*Sally R*

Bill's great attitude sets him on the course for healing. Even if he gets down, it sounds like he has the vision and the hope for beating this. It's got to be a lot of scariness. I truly believe that God is a God of miracles and I think you and Bill are due for some miracles.

—*Sue*

Triple Threat

March 20, 2018

Radiation + Chemo + Strong Will = Triple Threat to Cancer!

Bill's new protocol adds once a week chemo to daily radiation. Added to Bill's tough resolve, the plan is up and running. Today he got the first infusion from a different family of chemo. Now he will have radiation and we'll go home. As much as we miss everyone in Michigan, our Wisconsin spot is close, homey, and perfect for our needs right now.

> *I believe you have a Quadruple Threat........ add in the Holy Spirit and cancer will be knocked out cold!*
>
> *—Sally R*

The Big Yuck

March 21, 2018

We've discovered that radiation *and* chemo on the same day really make you feel lousy. Bill got up this morning and said, "I don't think I can go." There was plenty of time for more rest and after he got up for the second time, he agreed to power through and off we went. Brave guy, this man I love! Let's hope these combo days get easier.

Keep fighting the good fight, Bill. You have many people pulling for you and praying!

—Barbara

What a bummer cancer is and then to have two treatments in one day that knock your socks off makes it even worse. I think of both of you often and pray that God gives you the strength, courage, and fortitude to get through all of this. When he leads you to it - he'll lead you through it. Stay positive and hopeful.

—Luana

Just remember all of us are with both of you as you make this journey. We are hanging in there because we know together, we can do this. I know it is easy to say when on the outside but both of you are pillars of strength and make all of us stronger by your example.

—Louann

Your title, "The Big Yuck" says it all. Bravo for both of you for powering through. Prayers always!

—Sue

Good Better Best

March 22, 2018

Heat on my back: That feels *good*.

A dose of pain meds: I feel *better*.

Before bedtime: This is the *best* I've felt all day.

Who knew the old ratings for mattresses from the Sears and Roebuck catalog would sum up the day?

> *Glad you ended the day in the best possible way....but up very early.*
> *—Louann*

> *Take care of yourself, but remember God has this for both of you. One day at a time, one foot in front of another, even baby steps are OK. Praise God for the good days and moments.*
> *—Pam L*

The Still Small Voice of God

March 23, 2018

Yesterday was rough for Bill. It seems I'm reporting this quite a bit these days. After chemo and radiation on Tuesday, Bill felt like he collided with a truck in the middle of the road. It was *just* a radiation day. Hah-just! Maybe it's the cumulative work of all these treatments, but Bill felt pretty punky. He slept quite a bit, watched some basketball, and we headed to bed. Bill said he prayed like he does at bedtime and after a little while, and a peaceful calm filled him. I could hear the awe in his voice as he spoke. He said he has a firm belief that God is at work in him. The prayers of so many buoy him up. It's easy to feel sucked down by evil or enemy forces, but clearly, last night the assurance of God's hand was present. Singing praises this beautiful sunny morning.

> *In spite of the physical things he, and you, are enduring, there is something greater at work and he was able, in his sick and tired state to feel that presence. We are a very strong team Wright.*
>
> *—Louann*

> *When I was feeling so depleted caring for my parents in Frankenmuth, I had reached the end of my energy. I was driving back to Freeland and literally felt uplifted by prayer and the power of the Holy Spirit. In those few moments, I was "renewed in strength". Words do not explain, but the feelings were real. Praise God for peace and renewed strength for Bill.*
>
> *—Linda S*

> *We serve such an amazing God! Those quiet moments with the Father are some of His very favorite times to bless, calm, speak to, and reassure His children! We will not cease in our prayers and we will not quit believing and claiming this victory. He is in charge and doing amazing things every single day. Bill's faithfulness, even in the midst of pain and physical let-downs, is so strong. He is rewarded for his faithfulness. Grace unending. Claim it. Hugs.*
>
> *—Sally R*

> *There are no words to explain the healing presence of God. I am so happy to know that Bill felt His grace, love and peace. We are never alone. Prayers go out for both of you.*
>
> *—Diane*

When I was going through cervical cancer twenty six years ago, I felt my first real experience of God and again when I survived the accident. But Bernie, my husband, did not. I wish it didn't take tragedies to hear and feel the presence of God most pointedly. Continued prayers for more moments of Godly support.

—Debbie L

Wow! Prayers that you both get through these weeks with peace and comfort. It must seem like you're moving a boulder up a mountain.

—Sue

Something for Everyone

March 23, 2018

As I read comments from those of you who visit the Caring Bridge© site, I'm struck by the powerful testimonies from so many. How uplifting, not just for those of us *on* the journey, but those who have been, and witness in their postings the wonder and mystery of this faith walk. I hope those visiting the site read these hopeful words and stories. We are *never* alone! Physical presence is merely a detail. A community of wounded healers travels with us— sometimes step by step— and sometimes leaning in to give us support.

Thankful for these blessings.

> *I do read the other posts and am so thankful for a loving, always present Lord. Your road has not been easy but knowing He is with you through all of this is wonderful. Prayers continuing.*
>
> *—Cherryl*

> *Yes, I do read others posts. Hope you are buoyed by them. Prayers.*
>
> *—Ginny*

> *The strength you both are bringing to this "fight" is so powerful to watch and share. As Dr. Evans says pancreatic cancer only happens to good people. I am thankful for the goodness in you both!*
>
> *—Linda, Marcia's sister*

> *I've been wanting to share the "In Touch" app. I start my day listening to Dr. Stanley and I love it. Hope you enjoy it as much as I do. God bless you and Bill with strength and peace. Blessings. Love and hugs.*
>
> *—Lisa D*

What a Difference a Week Makes

March 25, 2018

Last Sunday, Bill and I went for a walk and Aaron and his friend joined us for dinner. This Sunday Bill feels miserable. He's extremely tired, nauseated, battling hydration and digestive issues, and feels discouraged. Doctors told him he won't feel the effects of chemo and radiation until he is halfway through treatment or even later. Well, they were wrong. The nursing staff at the 24 Hour Cancer Center paged the on call oncologist who believes it *is* the double treatment that's kicking him from here to next week. Hopefully we can get some intervention in place tomorrow when we go for radiation.

In the words of singers Sonny and Cher: "The Beat Goes On"*. (***Sonny Bono, Warner/Chappel Music, Inc. 1967**)

Just hang on because for every setback, God has a comeback.

—*Dawn*

So sorry to hear that treatments are so rough on Bill—-and you. I pray the doctor will come up with a solution to ease all of his discomfort. I'm glad you have family there to be with you and that you have someone to lean on. I miss your bright outfits, your smile, and your positive attitude at choir. Think of you often.

—*Luana*

So, so sorry to hear of the discomfort Bill is struggling with. And what about you? It's tough to watch a loved one suffer. I pray tomorrow will be a better day.

—*Margaret*

Such tough stuff for you both. Really tough stuff. Prayers for the oncology team to find interventions which give Bill some relief. Cancer treatment is so brutal. Prayers for both of you for strength and comfort through this time.

—*Julie S*

Life's A Roller Coaster

March 26, 2018

Following Bill's radiation treatment, we have a weekly consult with the radiation oncologist. I have a list of questions all starting with "why?" It will be really helpful if we hear the word "because" followed by explanations that are encouraging or say it's just "part of the process." That would be so much more hopeful instead of a decline of any sort. The journal postings last week were more upbeat and hopeful and here I am *again*, letting fear lock out faith.

P. S. Having just seen the doctor for a weekly check in, we learned that these miserable side effects *are* just that— how Bill is responding to the chemo and radiation. So we continue to pray for gentler times.

> *I hope you get some positive feedback from the report and get the answers you need to hear soon. I don't know that I would call it fear. I would call it concern and love for the #1 person in your life. I know you met with another couple who went through the same thing. Can you touch base with them to see if this is "normal" for this stage of treatment? Maybe you wouldn't feel so alone in this process if they could tell you how it goes, what they felt and that things will get better. Love and prayers sent your way today and every day.*
>
> —Luana

> *I hope you get some answers for the "whys." There is much to be fearful about. I think you can be fearful and hopeful at the same time. You and Bill are both bright, articulate people. They should be able to answer your questions.*
>
> —Sue

> *Hope you can get much needed information. I can't imagine the rollercoaster you both are on. Keep the faith. Prayers.*
>
> —Ginny

> *Journeys often present nasty bumps in the road and occasional potholes! I will be praying for a smoother road for traveling. Love to you both.*
>
> —Sally P

On Edge Waiting

March 27, 2018

Tuesday's agenda hit a snag. Bill had a blood draw before chemo and now we've been waiting for over half an hour to start chemo. When we checked with the staff, they said they would page the doctor because something "flagged" in his bloodwork. That's the hold up. Hopefully Bill can still have chemo. Radiation is scheduled in less than two hours.

> *Jesus—right now—step in and take charge. We need Your guidance and Your grace…as only You can provide. Amen!*
>
> *—Sally R*

> *Earnestly praying for you both right now. The Great Physician is in charge of Bill and his treatment. We are praying that all necessary communication among the members of Bill's team will take place with a clear direction on how to proceed. We are praying that you both have faith in the process and in the Holy Spirit to guide the process. We send our love and belief that God is still in charge.*
>
> *—Linda S*

Mission Accomplished

March 27, 2018

Things improved after the delay this morning. The doctors conferred and approved a modified chemo dose for this week. All of the coordinating from oncology and radiology took a little time. (What? You mean there are *other* patients who need care too?) So, as of now Bill has had:

- ✓ Anti-nausea treatment and chemo
- ✓ Fluid infusion
- ✓ Radiation
- ✓ A drive home
- ✓ A turkey sandwich

- ✓ And a nap: about to commence

Until tomorrow.

> *Each of you rest in the loving arms of the lord Jesus, constant thoughts and prayers from your sister. Oh, I love you.*
> —*Carolyn and Jim, Bill's sister and brother-in-law*
>
> *Praying for only good results for the two of you! Prayers from our church family also! Hope you have a blessed and happy Easter!*
> —*Dianna*

Kicking Cancer is Tough

March 28, 2018

The goal of chemotherapy and radiation before surgery is to shrink and/or kill the nasty cells in Bill's body. Giving it the old "knockout punch" sums up the action—and we are all for that! But cancer isn't the only thing suffering from the pummeling. Bill is one tired and beat up guy. After radiation today we talked to the nurse and doctor because he feels so lousy. They sent him to the Day Hospital for a two hour infusion. The rooms are very nice: private with the choice of a bed or recliner and even TV. Bill climbed into the bed, got hooked up to his IVs and fell asleep. Two hours later he felt a little better. We drove home, had a late lunch, and Bill went back to bed. Life isn't very exciting right now but it's so important to remember the means justifies the end result: a cure. And a little bonus for the day— we ran into our new friends from Michigan who were also there for an infusion. It must be that's where all the cool people hang out.

Your positive attitude is going to carry you a long way, Marcia. Do they have a library where you can get some books to take you away to other places for a while or can't you keep your mind on anything right now? If you can, get the book - The Impossible by Joyce Smith. It is a true story about prayers and miracles. Prayers always.

—Luana

Great idea, Luana! And, another good book, Marcia- In His Steps . It's about living a life truly asking "What would Jesus do?" and how it impacted an entire town! Hang in there— I'm still holding fervent prayers every morning for you both. Faithful, one day at a time— all He asks! And you both are doing a great job of it! Love and hugs!

—Sally R

I hope Bill is able to get a ton of sleep and that you can rest. Getting through each day right now must be so very difficult, but as you said, the prize at the end is the cure. Keep your eyes on the prize.

—Sue

Sleep is a wonderful medicine. You both have huge support from so many family and friends. Prayers continue. Take care.

—Cherryl

Bill's Entourage

March 29, 2018

Side effects are awful but the follow up to those concerns is meticulous. Bill felt lousy yesterday and saw some of the staff who consulted with his doctors (yes, his own team) and they sent him directly for fluids. During radiation the technician told Bill he would meet with his radiation oncologist afterward to follow up on how he feels today— it's not just "letting the doctor know" around here, but a frequent face to face. Radiation is meticulous: he has the same machine for every treatment, the same team of qualified technicians, and is carefully monitored by the radiologist who often checks in during his treatment to make sure everything is as she has instructed. This is the culture at the Cancer Center/ Medical College of Wisconsin. They really cater to patient care. With all of the stress cancer treatment causes, this is wonderful and reassuring.

> *Yes, so nice to have a consistent team who is there to help you. My husband Larry also had that and it's very comforting seeing people you get to know and they get to know you. As hard as it is, hang in there and focus on beating the cancer. Angels are everywhere, know you have many. Hugs and prayers to you both and your families.*
>
> —*Pam L*

> *Bill and Marcia- you certainly made the very best decision possible to relocate near Milwaukee and receive such wonderful care from your "team." Our precious Lord is watching out for you both by holding you in the palm of his hands. We miss you.*
>
> —*Margaret*

> *Simply great news and just have to add that your caregivers get as much back from you two as they give. We know the whiners, complainers, Debbie Downers who see nothing good and you two, in spite of some areas that need more attention continue to be open, receptive, thankful, positive. We all know it is a two way street with you and the team, and going side by side is so much more productive and beneficial for all. So thank them and also kudos to you, too, for being open and doing this in spite of the sickness, physical and mental. You two are the best example... ... .just my take as I read this.*
>
> —*Louann*

Lending a Hand

March 30, 2018

Bill's radiation oncologist asked him if he would be willing to participate in some research that will benefit pancreatic cancer patients in the future. Once a week after radiation, he has an advanced imaging procedure on a MR Linac (Electa) –it's brand new and gives the doctors a better image of the cancer before and during radiation. The images that will be obtained when Bill is in the scanner will help to fine tune the images for future patients who will be treated on the MR Linac and will also be analyzed for some information within the images that may give clues about how the cancer is responding to radiation. They will start using it here next year. It's voluntary and won't benefit Bill but he said, "If I can help one person in some small way with this horrible cancer, I am glad to do this." Just another reason why I love this man so much.

> *Why am I not surprised about the response from you or Bill? What a gift you are bringing to all who try to walk the tightrope balance of life between hopefulness and fearfulness. Thank you for bringing so much light.*
>> *Loads of love, prayers and blessings always!*
>
> *—Pat S*

> *God bless you, Bill. Somehow it's a comfort to feel like you might be able to help others someday just as you are being helped from others that have gone through this ahead of you. Thank you*
>> *—Pam L*

> *It brought tears to my eyes to think that Bill in this tough situation has thought to help others with this horrible disease. Who knows who he might be helping in the future?*
>> *—Sue*

> *Bill has a beautiful soul and you two are a such blessing. God Bless you guys*
>> *—Lisa D*

This sounds just like Bill, willing to help others as needed. I am so proud of both of you for this long journey. You both have always faced new challenges, seized new opportunities, tested your resources against the unknown and in the process, discovered your own unique potential. Always remember, nothing in life is to be feared. It is only to be understood. **Psalm 91:4 (NIV)** reads "He will cover you with His feathers, and under His wings you will find refuge; His faithfulness will be your shield and rampart." May God bless both of you this Easter season!

—Dianna

All Quiet on the Western Front

March 31, 2018

Saturdays at the Day Hospital are very quiet compared to the busy week days at the Cancer Center. Bill is getting fluid infusions three days a week to keep him hydrated (Tuesdays, Thursdays, Saturdays). It takes over two hours and today when we go home we will see Zac who is coming for Easter along with Aaron, who will be with us, too. It will be so nice to have some family with us.

> *Marcia, you have a talent for titles!*
> *We are glad to know that you will have family with you this weekend. Easter*
> *is a day of joy and hope. May it be so for you and Bill.*
> *Take care.*
>
> —*Julie S*

> *Enjoy your precious time together, praying you both will have a good day.*
> *Blessings*
>
> —*Pam L*

> *Have a blessed Easter and enjoy your time with the family.*
>
> —*Sue*

> *Wishing you the peace and joy of this Easter celebration. May your faith and*
> *strength be replenished by the miracle of His resurrection.*
>
> —*Linda S*

> *What a nice Easter with family there! Wonder if the bunny will be able to*
> *smuggle in some candy? Enjoy the time as family.*
>
> —*Louann*

"Spoiler Alert: The Tomb was Empty"

April 1, 2018

I saw that slogan on a t shirt and thought it was fantastic. What a tremendous way to think about Easter morning! Exposure to germs kept us from church but we had our kids visiting so it was great to have time with them. We fixed a ham dinner. Sadly, Bill was under the weather and couldn't join us. We all enjoyed watching the Final Four basketball game on TV last night so maybe that was too much excitement adding to his troubles today. He spent most of the day resting in bed but did get up in the early afternoon to visit with the kids before they went their respective ways. Now he's back in bed sleeping and hopefully it will settle his pain and discomfort. Easter blessings to you all.

> *Marcia and Bill...I saw a shirt that said "April Fool's"....... and it had the tomb with the stone rolled away! Another good one! Day by day mode for you both. So glad family was here to celebrate Easter with you. Ya'll are "doing family" and "doing life" as it comes, and as it works best for you in this season...My prayer for you as you start the week: remember that He calls us by name. When Mary saw Jesus the first time at the tomb, He called her by name! Live this week knowing the King of Kings knows you by name! And that you can take to the bank! Love you both and just know that you are consistently and fervently prayed for every single morning! We are claiming little victories on the path toward healing.*
>
> *—Sally R*

> *Family, basketball, simple pleasures. Good spirit boosts! Prayers for this week. May these tough treatments do their work. Hugs to you both!*
>
> *—Julie S*

"Weak" Three Begins

April 2, 2018

Bill is one tuckered out guy and this is his third week of the radiation chemo combo. By the end of the week he will be over the half way mark with this rigorous course of treatment, the Final Four tournament will have crowned a champ, and the Masters golf tournament will be underway. There's good stuff ahead!

> *Again, as crummy as he feels, seems like that is what they know and expect to happen so we know it is doing just what it is supposed to do—kill the cause! Half way is great: half a school year, pregnancy, book, means we are looking at the end of a journey and not the onset. All will be fine and some sports on the tube for a minor diversion!*
>
> *—Louann*

> *Praying for good stuff, healing, less tired, strength, hope, and less worries for both of you ahead. Blessings to you friends.*
>
> *—Pam L*

> *Hang in there. The Lord is giving you both strength to see this through. Prayers to keep you both in His loving care. Hugs.*
>
> *—Cherryl*

> *I love your clever titles. You and Bill are certainly champs. We continue to send positive thoughts your way.*
>
> *—Margaret*

> *Marcia, you have a way with words. Look forward to your messages. Happy Bill is almost halfway through this wave of treatment. Prayers!*
>
> *—Ginny*

> *Keep leaning on his strength and love........ the more we need it, the more is given.*
>
> *—Carolyn and Jim, Bill's sister and brother-in-law*

NO CHEMO FOR YOU!

April 3, 2018

A la Seinfeld's Soup Nazi: No Chemo for Bill. Blood levels are too low which explains some of the malaise he's experiencing. While the chemo helps the radiation work better, it's a tough course of treatment. Apparently this is a common occurrence. So today he gets fluids, radiation, and a consult with Dr. Evans, his surgeon. Tomorrow he has a weekly meeting with his radiation oncologist, has radiation (including the voluntary procedure), and meets with the oncologist who will take more blood and assess whether levels are going up. If so, the week off chemo may be just what his body needs to recover a bit.

> *Almost past midpoint. Grateful for the very attentive care Bill is receiving. Hope Bill feels better this week. Blessings!*
> *—Julie S*

> *I know it's awful to be there, but it sounds like they are taking super good care of Bill. I don't think you could be in a better place.*
> *—Sue*

> *That first time counts are too low can be upsetting, but it is NOT uncommon. I remember that with my son, Kurt. The counts will improve— that just takes time. From everything you have posted, he is receiving excellent care.*
> *—Linda L*

> *Sounds like Bill is being well taken care of. Hope he feels better this week and can continue on the program. Now you need to take care of yourself. Blessings!*
> *—Ginny*

Knock Knock. Who's there?

April 4, 2018

Today is a long day of waiting. After labs early this morning, the radiation oncology schedule was running behind. They sent us to another oncology clinic for an appointment and they, too, were behind. We went back to radiation oncology. Still behind. We waited. Oncology said come back after the radiation oncology appointment, but radiation oncology was still behind. We were told, "The doctors really want to see you." By 1:30 (the time we *should* have been finished), we were still waiting in radiation oncology not knowing if radiation would happen. Bill is so tired and has had nothing to eat or drink (per orders for labs and radiology). Frustrated? A bit, I'd say— when a good nap would be so helpful as we sit in very firm upright chairs— still waiting.

> Knock knock.
> Who's there?
> Nobody.
> Nobody who?
> Nobody seems to be on time today.

So frustrating I'm sure. Praying all these bumpy roads will soon be behind you and you both will share a beautiful rainbow as you walk hand in hand with years of good health ahead.

—Pam L

Oh my, you surely did not need all that waiting and back and forth stuff—so sorry. Sure do hope this finds you +back in your cozy condo nest recouping from such an exhaustive day. Rest. God bless.

—Julie S

My prayer tonight is that the staff will be back at the top of their form tomorrow and that you two will have smooth sailing through the day.

—Linda S

Weary Platelets

April 5, 2018

After a day with lots of inertia, it got worse. Bill's platelets are dangerously low - 17,000 (normal range is 165,000-360,000). He cannot have chemo this week and radiation is off the table until the levels are above 20,000. His bone marrow, the doctor stated, "is worn out" from cumulative chemotherapy. The white blood cells, lower Tuesday and up slightly on Wednesday, have begun to rebound though—a good sign. Oncology sent him to have a platelet infusion yesterday. That can artificially raise the platelet count and hopefully his body will begin to make more on its own. He's also off all blood thinners because there is a huge risk of bleeding. We got home around 6:15 PM thinking we would have been home much earlier.

But around 4:00 AM this morning, Bill said "I feel pretty good!" Thank you, Lord! He's just had another blood test to see how the transfusion worked and if it shows a significant rise in the platelet count, he can have radiation. We are waiting with expectancy.

> *Thank you Lord for a tiny relief...bless you both with strength and a little more good news.*
> *—Carolyn and Jim, Bill's sister and brother-in-law*

> *Tough, tough stuff. So glad he felt a little better. Prayers for positive news.*
> *—Julie S*

> *You both are my heroes. My admiration grows with each bit of news. God's love is the constant in all of this. Prayers unceasing for you.*
> *—Sally P*

> *Thank you Lord. The highs and lows of your journey. Prayers.*
> *—Ginny*

YES!

April 5, 2018

A simple message: radiation is a go! Platelets jumped to 36,000. Thank God from whom all blessings flow!

Wonderful news!! Prayers are continuing. God is good!!
—Cherryl

So happy, may they continue to rise. May Bill feel better with that rise and that the radiation kills the cancer cells. Yes, many blessings flow! Prayers.
—Pam

God continues to bless both of you! May you continue on this journey with him by your side always!!
—Dianna

Good news! May Bill's platelet levels continue to rise. God's peace, love and healing continue to be with you on your journey.
—Diane

Praise Him all creatures here below!
—Amy, Marcia's sister

Praise Father, Son and Holy Ghost!
—Dawn

Praise of the platelets and prayers for all of you.
—Louann

Fantastic News! Prayers continue for more good news.
—Julie S

Your last few posts remind me of the one and only roller coaster ride I ever took. I am so thankful you have invited us to share this ride with the two of you. We are praising God for answered prayer today.
—Linda L

Wahoo!
Our God is an awesome God! So, so thrilled for you all! What a blessing! One step closer!
—Sally R

Wonderful News!!
Blessings!
—Marcia L

Checks and Balances and Family

April 6, 2018

My sister Linda and husband Steve arrived from Chicago last night. Linda brought dinner and booted me out of the kitchen when it was clean up time. It was so thoughtful and a real treat—she's a great cook. It's great to have them here because they are both so supportive. They graciously went with us to Bill's appointments, too. The time passed more quickly and the happy distraction was welcome.

The platelets were up some more today so radiation was on schedule— putting Bill at the halfway mark! After that he met with the radiation oncologist and nurse to discuss how he was feeling. Attentive care from the medical staff helps keep us on track.

> *Glad you are all able to be together and support one another Food for the body and the soul arrived, it appears. Halfway sounds great on the trek. As always thoughts and prayers heading to Badgerland for all.*
>
> *—Louann*

> *I'm so glad you have some angels with you! Also glad that Bill has reached the halfway point on this journey.*
>
> *—Sue*

> *How nice to have family close and willing to cook too. That is awesome. Things are looking up for you and Bill. Our prayers continue. God bless you both.*
>
> *—Julie S*

> *It's so nice to have family support and how awesome they were able to keep you company during the appointments!! So glad to hear you are halfway through. Prayers continue!! Hugs!!*
>
> *—Cherryl*

> *Always nice to have family not too far away. While Bill doesn't feel good, it sounds like his results are improved. Here's to continued progress!*
>
> *—Nancy H*

Saturday's Change of Plans

April 7, 2018

The doctors added Saturday back into Bill's schedule for additional fluids. At least that *was* the plan for today, but his body told him otherwise. Travel to the Day Hospital was more than he felt he could handle even though it's a short ride in the car. The world of pancreatic cancer *and* this stage of radiation make it hard to feel safe for car travel. I'm hoping the two days off from treatment will make Monday a sure thing and put him back on track.

It's a good thing the televised Masters tournament offered an enjoyable diversion today.

> *Prayers for rest and feeling better for Bill and freedom from worry for you.*
> *—Sue*

> *Thank you, Marcia, for your updates! We continue to keep Bill and you in our prayers and hope that the weekend's rest will give him the strength for Monday's treatment. Sending hugs!!*
> *—Nancy B*

> *Let's hope rest this weekend will make it easier for Bill on Monday. Hope one of Bills favorites, too, is still in contention at the Masters. Take care of yourself. Prayers.*
> *—Ginny*

Sunday: A Day of Rest

April 8, 2018

It's a quiet day for Bill. He's very weary with no appetite. The dietician gave us a very specific list of foods to eat/not to eat. Those with fiber are off the list along with many fruits and vegetables that are favorites. Everything has an adverse effect so we're treading lightly with menu planning. Tomorrow is a lab/bloodwork day, weekly check in with the doctor, and if blood levels are stable or increasing—radiation. We truly hope we can get some input for nutrition that will be satisfying for Bill. Life in mashed "potatoville" is rather boring.

Did I Hear 100,000? Woot Woot!

April 9, 2018

Platelets are a whopping 100,000 flirting with the threshold of *normal*! Bill had radiation and saw his radiation oncologist for a weekly check in. They are very conscientious here and he has seen her *more* than once a week due to his complications. We are in the right spot for treatment. Dr. Erickson (radiation oncologist) is consulting with a partnering oncologist to help manage side effects Bill's experiencing. They have a care team who offer tips for nutrition management— so that is on the agenda, too. All of these strategies support that important preparation for surgery. Dr. Evans, his surgeon, wants Bill as healthy as possible before he has the operation. We've also learned that in the month after radiation and chemo finish, Bill will have *pre*-habilitation. With a physical therapist, he will participate in a work out designed to build strength and stamina. Bill is so excited about this possibility and because he brought his bicycle, he's hoping to do some shorter cycling, too, on the biking paths around us. So while a calmer belly would be nice, we know we are moving in that direction and will have some help achieving that soon.

> *Good news out there—-finally. Sounds like this place is phenomenal. I'm so glad you were able to find it and have the where-with-all to go, to stay and to have such wonderful care.*
> —*Luana*

> *Every day is a new day. It's wonderful to hear how special Bill is being treated even with the highs and lows. You definitely are in the right place. Thank you, Marcia, for the updates. We sure miss you. Praying for you both.*
> —*Margaret*

> *What wonderful news! Sounds like an absolutely state of the art facility and caring, compassionate people! Pedal on, Bill! Your support team is cheering you on!*
> —*Marcia L*

Business as Usual

April 10, 2018

I have the pleasure of reporting that today was normal— that is, the *new* normal. Labs/chemo/ and radiation all went like clockwork. Bill got a nap during chemo in a reasonably comfy bed with warm blankets and we went home.

No sooner did we arrive, the power went out. Happily we were off the elevator. A power surge took out the new range but the beauty of renting means someone else fixes it. The microwave worked perfectly for dinner and Bill is sound asleep— doing just what he needs to do.

> *Bless your hearts....... a little respite can be a peaceful release.*
> *—Carolyn and Jim, Bill's sister and brother-in-law*

> *You should write a book.*
> *—Margaret*

> *I'm so glad that today went well overall. The two of you deserve as many good breaks as possible. I'm also glad you didn't get stuck in the elevator. That would have been so tiring for both of you.*
> *—Sue*

> *Hope you follow with sleep time for you...am sure you are as exhausted as he is.*
> *—Louann*

A Busy Man

April 11, 2018

Today Bill had radiation, a consult with his radiation oncologist, the research scan for his voluntary project, and set up appointments with physical therapy for next week to design a program for strength building. And, because they monitor what patients eat (or don't eat), a care team will also do a consult next week. Thursday is stacking up to be a *busy* day. Bill grumbled, "I'll be here all day!"

That's what you get for being so popular.

> *Sounds like Bill is getting good attention— probably more than he'd like. Stay strong and take care of yourself.*
>
> *—Ginny*

> *Your disposition continues to teach and preach, missy! So proud of how you both are finding joy in the moment, as that is always a choice! You both have risen up to the challenge and faced it head on! We have not slowed our fervent prayers for you, and you can count on the daily direct line of communication we have available to us straight to God through His Son. Lean in, hang on, and count on the Holy Spirit to uplift, hold up, and carry you both daily. I look forward to your updates as they keep us connected when we cannot be there with you. Love and big ole hugs from me to you both today! Chin up, rise up, and choose to "be" up! Hugs.*
>
> *—Sally R*

> *All sounds better and your dance cards are filling up for the week. You are missing some snowflakes here— yay Spring.*
>
> *—Louann*

> *You both must get so weary from all of the appointments, but each one has to be a building block for recovery!*
>
> *—Sue*

A World of Its Own

April 13, 2018

The Cancer Center on the campus of the Medical College of Wisconsin is a huge five story building surrounded by parking structures, a regular hospital, the Center for Advanced Care, and many other medical buildings. The second and third floors of the Cancer Center are where most of the action takes place for us. The third floor houses the Day Hospital along with radiation oncology.

Downstairs, on the second floor are the clinics, labs, gift shop and a bistro for breakfast and lunch—where the food is pretty good. The common spaces are carpeted and the colors are muted earth tones— all to create calmness. Floor to ceiling windows fill three of the four exterior walls on this floor creating lots of natural light and views of green spaces, mature trees, ponds, and the Milwaukee skyline. It's all very pleasant and lends nicely to the purposeful intent of keeping things tranquil. After all, everyone here either has cancer or loves someone who does.

A walking path for patients (or those trying to be "patient") surrounds the perimeter of this floor. The clinics are called Peace, Courage, Serenity, and Faith in large flowing graphics. At first I thought it was kind of corny to have names for the clinics— but now I'm understanding. As you walk these words visually "speak" as reminders for those who are on a very difficult journey.

Entering from the parking structure, there are nature sounds (crickets, frogs, birds chirping, and water gurgling) with visuals of creatures from nature. Not only does it help orient you to your parking spot, it sets the tone for serenity. (And there are small business cards color coded by all elevators for visitors to take as reminders in case they are preoccupied when they first arrive.)

Cancer is a horrible, ugly disease. So much of who you are is destroyed in the process of diagnosis and treatment. Fear and uncertainty taunt you. Your faith is challenged and you learn to be stronger than you ever thought you could. Being in a setting like this, if you have to, is a little easier and a bit more soothing to these fragile souls.

I just read an article recently that said God has mapped out our life for us. We may not know where (or why) our map will take us, but God does. He will never leave us but gives us His love and the love of family and friends along the way. Prayers continue. Hugs!!

—Cherryl

Thank you for the wonderful description of the cancer center. It helps us visualize where you are. We are happy that it is a calm and comfortable environment for you both. Sending our love and daily prayers.

—Linda S

It sounds as though things at this center are working together to help make this journey as easy as possible, even though it is anything but easy. So grateful you have found a place where the whole person is treated. Hugs and continued prayers.

—Linda L

The description of the hospital environment shows the thoughtfulness that goes into the treatment of all the cancer families who are there. It is reassuring to know you are both in a place where your needs are being met with care and love. It makes you feel that God is reassuring you in many ways. Prayers for you both.

—Diane

Your beautiful description came through to my email a little after 3:00 am. I hope that doesn't mean that you weren't able to sleep. Cancer is a journey that no one ever wants to be on. As you know, it's a horrible disease in which the treatments can be as bad as the disease. I pray that you and Bill get on the recovery side of this as soon as possible.

—Sue

Praying that you are breathing in those beautiful words: peace – courage— serenity— during this faith walk you are on.

—Amy, Marcia's sister

Opting Out of Winter

April 14, 2018

It may be spring according to the calendar but the weather is horrible. We have sleety rain, cold, and *lots* of wind. Our "homies" in Michigan report severe winter storms across the northern part of the state. We say "Enough! Let the nice weather begin."

Last night we celebrated Aaron's birthday here with Angel Food cake that was so light we had to weigh it down with candles.

Saturday was a "fluids" day for Bill, but again, travel to the Day Hospital was a bit iffy— so he stayed home which was a great choice. Figuring out what foods are satisfying and don't wreak havoc when your pancreas is performing poorly is trial and error— lots of error. And it is very trying for poor Bill. He eats very little and very little sounds tasty— a real frustration because weight maintenance is critical for optimum radiation and preparation for surgery. So, we try different things hoping to hit on the right combination and once in a while we get lucky.

Monday is a weekly check in with the doctor and we may get more insight then. Later in the week, we have a consult with the care team and they, too, may have ideas to help with things related to food. In the meantime, I am stress eating for both of us! I may return to Michigan much more than a shadow of my former self.

> *Prayers that you'll find some answers to the eating and nutrition. I have no idea what Bill's likes and restrictions are, but when my mom was having radiation, she wanted homemade rice pudding. My culinary skills are sorely lacking, but with her verbal guidance I was able to do a decent rice pudding.*
> *—Sue*

> *Hope that you can get some helpful advice from the staff. These are tough challenges but so thankful that Aaron is around and you could celebrate his birthday together. Prayers continue from our home to yours. Take good care.*
> *—Julie S*

A Tiny View of the Finish Line

April 16, 2018

No radiation today. The software that "talks" to the radiation equipment crashed and they are working feverishly to get it up and running. Bill just does not have it in him to wait. It was a Herculean effort to shower and get in the car amid the snow this morning to go to the Cancer Center. So, we had a consult with the doctor who was encouraging about Bill doing all the right things as a patient— and went home. It will extend treatment one day but we can still say "*next* week Bill finishes chemo and radiation." It might seem a bit early to start with these rally cries but it's such a rough trek right now and being able to anticipate and think about a glimmer of finishing this treatment buoys us up mentally.

> *We are counting the days and treatments with you all the way....so many challenges already completed.......*
> *Karma and love from snowy Glen Ellyn.*
>
> *—Linda, Marcia's sister*

> *You've come so far and being able to say "next week Bill finishes chemo and radiation" is wonderful. Take care and prayers continuing.*
>
> *—Cherryl*

> *It's a long journey to the end of the tunnel but it's okay to see a glimmer of light. We think of you daily.*
>
> *—Margaret*

> *Yahoo! I know that there are challenges ahead but this step is such a victory, through God everything is possible. Praying for strength for each of you. Time to plan a party even if it's a sigh of relief! Peace be with you Bill and Marcia.*
>
> *—Pam L*

> *That finish line is in view and I'm sure you can see it!! After next week, everything will be positively keyed toward physical improvement and not anything detrimental to your body...WOW!! What a blessing! Soon....very soon, you will have that shriveled up growth of dead cancer cells taken out. What a blessing........... Hang in there and look at that beautiful finish line... You deserve it. We love you both.*
>
> *—Carolyn and Jim, Bill's sister and brother-in-law*

Marcia and Bill, I'm glad to hear the good news! It sounds like you are in the right place for treatment. This has been a very long journey for both of you, Remember when either of you get down you have a strong team back home praying for this great victory! God will always be by your side no matter what! Take care of yourselves and hope to see you back in Michigan real soon. God bless both of you!

—Dianna

Yes/No/Chemo-No

April 17, 2018

After labs this morning, Bill's neutrophils came back *very* low— meaning no chemo this week. That's good news/ bad news. Good: Bill won't be as sick. Bad: this chemo helps the radiation work more effectively. He needs higher numbers to get over the go/no go threshold and to ward off potential infection. At this stage of treatment, that's critical to monitor. So he's getting hydration fluids and will head to radiology for his treatment in a couple of hours. He's been given a comfy bed in a private treatment room, so guess what he's doing right now? Sleeping. It's very restorative.

In every situation of our journeys we can take one of two paths. I am continually proud of you for taking the path of finding the good. It is so much healthier for everyone. There are always "pockets of joy" in our days. Thanks for continuing to find yours!

—Sally R

Prayers for rest for both of you and that the radiation will do its mighty work despite not having the chemo. It's amazing how illness gives you a whole new set of words that you'd rather not learn. I had never heard of the word neutrophils until now and didn't realize how important they are.

—Sue

Continued prayers for both of you. Keep up the good fight and have patience. God will always have his hand on both of your shoulders as you continue on your wellness journey. God bless.

—Dianna

Your friend, Sally said it so perfectly. You continue to see the light in the shadows. I'm proud to know you. Prayers for you both.

—Diane

Ordinary is Sometimes the Best

April 18, 2018

Today was a predictable day. Radiation was uneventful. We headed home for some lunch and Bill said, "A grilled cheese sandwich sounds good." It was great news to hear something sounded appealing—so that's exactly what we had with homemade chicken noodle soup and all of it "settled" well.

Tomorrow is a very busy day: physical therapy consult, fluids, radiation, and a planning meeting with the care team to figure out ways to successfully manage side effects of treatment.

Ordinary, simple days like this make good respite amid all the intense treatment.

> Glad it was a "good" day!
>
> —Linda L

> Good day: check! Good lunch: check! Good spirit: check! Great and mighty God: CHECK!
>
> —Sally R

> I'm so glad to hear things went well today. You need some "good"… You have found such a wonderful team of doctors who seem to be taking such good care of Bill. Today was a one step forward day.
>
> —Luana

> Got to love a day when Bill thinks something would taste good and it did. May there be more days like this ahead for you. It was a grilled cheese type of day. Blessings and hugs!
>
> —Pam L

Like a Hamster Running on a Wheel

April 19, 2018

It was a crazy, busy day for Bill! He met with *pre*-habilitation staff to set up a strength building program for him before surgery. Dr. Evans recognizes his patients are pretty weary after chemo and radiation and advises rest and recovery for one month. So the program is in place with a combination of exercises and cardio workouts he can do at home and at the Cancer Center leading up to that important milestone.

Then he had radiation followed by two hours of fluids. Finally, we met with a care team to talk about ways to manage the side effects of radiation and chemo. While we didn't learn anything particularly new, we realized we're doing what we should be doing and much of where Bill is right now is due to all he's been through for the last six months. Needless to say, he conked out when we got home and is sound asleep in his spiffy recliner. I'm tiptoeing around just so he can rest.

Just *one* more week of treatment to go!

> *Sounds like Bill is on the right track. Happy he can sleep after such a big day. Stay strong and you get some rest!*
> —*Ginny*

> *One more week, seemed so far away at the outset but here you are! I love the pre-habilitation term.*
> —*Louann*

> *I didn't realize you only had a week left. You both have been doing so well. That doesn't mean we will stop praying or sending you our love and support. We are with you all the way.*
> —*Linda S*

On One Hand

April 20, 2018

After radiation today, Bill said, "I can count my remaining treatments on one hand."

Next week is very busy with appointments every day in multiple places but the caveat is that it's the last week of chemo/radiation. I'm excited (it doesn't take much) and I can only imagine how Bill must feel (tuckered out today... but knowing the bulk of this phase is behind him is such a relief).

The weekend is blissfully void of appointments *and* mild weather is in the forecast.

God is good!

> *Hoorah!!!! Enjoy a drive along the lake shore in the sunshine soon and listen for Spring peepers in the ponds :-) Goals are good. Goals reached are even better! Love and prayers always.*
> —*Pat S*

> *Blessings, how good it must feel to know part of this journey is almost done. Hope you get a chance to enjoy the spring like weather we are supposed to have this weekend even if it's to sit in a sunny window. Enjoy your weekend!*
> —*Pam L*

> *Wonderful news!! So happy for both of you to be near the end of these treatments. Hope you enjoy the weekend, the warmth and lots of hope ahead!*
> —*Barbara*

In the Blink of an Eye

April 22, 2018

As promising as Friday appeared, Saturday smacked Bill in the face. He was nauseated and it was difficult to find satisfying food. But, he rested and by bedtime last night, he did feel better. We tried some meditation through the Insight app on our phones which was very calming and soothing. Our friend and yoga teacher, Rita, introduced it to us some time ago but we have just forgotten to use it. Now that it is at the front of the memory file drawer, it will be a useful tool!

I did some shopping at the Container Store which is nearby and bought some items for home and travel. This is probably one of my favorite stores because they have truly made organization an art. (Truthfully, it's a stress busting activity for me to wander among the bins and tubs and shelf stacking items. Leave it to me to make this about shopping.)

Today is beautiful and promises to be warm. Hoping Bill will be up for a walk outside. A week ago it was snowing like crazy and now we are feeling the flirt of a spring breeze.

> *I hope you both are having a better day today. Shopping as a stress buster for illness sounds very right somehow.*
> *—Sue*

> *Hope Bill is better today and you can get a walk in. Both of you stay strong!*
> *—Ginny*

> *Praying that this new week goes very well—without any "hiccups". Thinking of you lots each day, dear friend!*
> *—Nancy B*

Utter Exhaustion

April 23, 2018

A very, very tired Bill Wright lies in the hospital bed as I write. After radiation this morning, he couldn't power through physical therapy so we went home for a couple hours and then back to the Cancer Center for fluids. As the IV drips, drips, drips into his port, he sleeps under those wonderful heated blankets. Next up, we go back home where Bill will undoubtedly occupy some horizontal space there, too. Hoping to entice him with "gourmet" white rice and bland vegetables for "dinner". The countdown has begun—four treatments to go!

> *You have to be exhausted too. Please get as much rest as you can. Better days ahead!*
> *—Ginny*

> *Bless you both...we are constantly thinking of you, caring about you, loving you, so close to a respite—rest and recuperation are just ahead*
> *—Carolyn and Jim, Bill's sister and brother-in-law*

> *I am counting the days down along with you. Take some much needed rest for yourself. Prayers continue.*
> *—Cherryl*

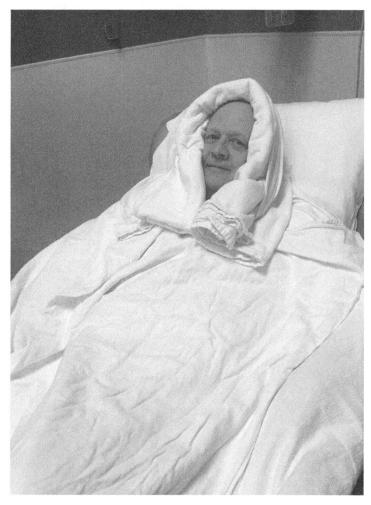

"Mummy" Bill, wrapped in warm blankets to offset the cold effects of chemo

Hip Hip Hooray! Last Chemo Day!

April 24, 2018

Bloodwork is all terrific this morning so chemo is a go for the last time! Wahoo! This is a view of the mummy wrap that keeps Bill's body warm while the chilly chemo infuses. Radiation follows this and then two consults: radiation oncology and surgery. It's a busy but productive day with just three more to go before the treatment finale.

> *Awesome news! "For the last time" sounds SO good!! Prayers continue.*
> *—Cherryl*

> *Wonderful, the countdown is on, even looks like you got a smile from Bill in his mummy wrap! You guys are doing a great job and what a wonderful feeling to know that God is walking with you. Prayers continue, God bless you both!*
> *—Pam L*

> *Sounds great, Bill you are a real trooper and Marcia you have been an excellent caregiver! May God continue to be with you on the rest of the journey!*
> *—Dianna*

> *Best news ever. You guys have been so strong with all this and it is not lost on me how much time you have spent keeping us informed of the journey. With all else going on, you both are true to yourselves in keeping your circle up to date. I'm sure there were many times when just getting through the day was more than enough and still you cared enough to keep the journal for us.*
> *—Louann*

"Fantastic"

April 24, 2018

Dr. Evans, Bill's gifted surgeon (and the reason we are here), proclaimed Bill in *fantastic* shape. He's really pleased with how well Bill has tolerated the ravages of this treatment and will schedule the surgery soon. I'm so proud of Bill and *all* he has endured. Even though the days have been rough he has maintained the courage, strength, determination and commitment to do what he has to do. During this "time off" between treatment and surgery, they want him to walk, walk, and walk…and do some exercises. This very strong man will become even stronger.

Got to love the pre-habilitation! Must be one of the many reasons things have gone as well as they have. You are so in the right place with how this is unraveling and looking forward to scheduling the surgery. Not sure there has been better news for both of you. The doc is lucky to have you guys as patients, as I am sure there are many who do not/cannot follow the outline to ensure the most success. You are all winners in Badgerland!

—Louann

This IS outstanding! Such a powerful statement of endurance, patience in the waiting, and determination! You BOTH are huge encouragement to those around you. My prayer for today is that you two celebrate the victory of today. Spend today IN today! Love and hugs to you both!!!! Wahoo!

—Sally

Brought tears to my eyes for many reasons, so happy for you both. Bill is doing his part with the program his doctors have planned for him. Marcia you are a wonderful caregiver, it's not always easy to be upbeat during these times. Together you stand tall, keep up the great work.

—Pam L

So good to hear he is coming through this battle in strong form and surgery is just around the corner. You are such a wonderful cheerleader for Bill and others, Marcia! Way to go! Happy for you both!

—Barbara

Waiting for the Door to Open

April 25, 2018

As I sit and wait for Bill, I'm reminded of how big this undertaking was at the beginning – much more so for Bill because of all he endured physically. But now, as he is getting one of the *last three* treatments, time seems to have flown. The support of all the Caring Bridge© followers, friends on Facebook, Instagram, cards in the mail, and the face to face contacts have strengthened us. The comments you've posted are so encouraging. Just as a marathoner reaches the end of a race, it becomes even more important to cheer and root for that runner. As Bill gets close to his finish line, your words give us courage and we thank you.

> *I care so much for both of you and it hurts me when it hurts you. You are in my thoughts and especially prayers daily and I hope you can feel them coming your way. The strong drug regimen is coming to an end and I hope Bill can gain strength each day and be ready for the next big hurdle.*
>
> *—Luana*

> *Hey, we are all in it to win it. You two are doing the real tough work but we are all "Bill and Marcia Strong" from the get go and will be ready to celebrate crossing the finish line!*
>
> *—Louann*

> *You have recruited a great "cheering section" for this marathon. I think we get much more than we give. You inspire us, make us think, make us laugh and cry and humble us with your strength and love for each other.*
> *Thank you for allowing us to share your adventure.*
>
> *—Linda S*

> *It's got to be like you've been running hurdles and even though the race isn't over, this huge part of it almost is.*
>
> *—Sue*

Big News!

April 26, 2018

Oddly, my hand is trembling as I enter this text. Surgery is scheduled for June 4th! It's a feeling of immense elation to know Bill is making it to that important juncture and knowing that tomorrow is the last radiation treatment makes this a huge day. He will have all of the month of May to regain strength and feel better. Weather should be good and conducive for this. Now comes the flurry of *other* appointments with various specialty clinics getting everything checked and aligned for the fight of Bill's life. God has blessed us with miracles along the way and you, our earthly angels and supporters, are steadfast with love and prayers that mean so much. As beautifully composed by Handel: "Hallelujah!"

> *June 4th it is, wonderful news, there are many of us earthly angels watching each and every step you've taken. You are, and will continue to be, in our prayers. Let's hope May is a month of regained strength mentally and physically.*
>
> *—Pam L*

> *Our God is an <u>awesome</u> God! Wow! So thrilled. There is such a long season in the waiting. You both have risen up, met it all head on, always letting God go first into every situation and now, now is your time!*
>
> *—Sally R*

> *It is really happening – it's on the calendar!! The day you've been waiting for. I'm sure it's very scary but Bill has persevered. Hope you can enjoy some warm sunshine in the meantime.*
>
> *—Margaret*

> *For the Lord God Omnipotent reigneth. Hallelujah! Tears of happiness for you both and for the power of prayer and the power of the living God.*
>
> *—Linda S*

> *Great news as the treatment moves forward, or as Dr. Evans said to us in that first appt. "We are going for the cure!" You will both be surrounded by love and prayers from all us –and many of us there with you in person.*
>
> *—Linda, Marcia's sister*

Full Circle

April 27, 2018

The radiation oncology clinic is its own microcosm of humanity. People come fearful of what lies ahead— there are so many unknowns. The schedules are established with planning, scans, models and the eventual treatments. Each day patients come and go— sometimes alone, sometimes with loved ones, and those who are incapacitated arrive with help from the hospital staff. This whole mixture of people settles into a living little hum of action and inertia. Occasionally you hear chimes and applause. Someone has finished their treatment and it's cause for celebration. Others stand at the registration desk as new patients unsure of what to do.

Technicians come to the waiting area doing their very best to smile and be encouraging as they collect their patients for treatment. As the days pass, familiarity builds. Patients banter lightly with their technicians— how they feel, what's new with them, casual conversations of near normalcy. They develop brief but trusting relationships with the people who oversee the precious treatment that's needed. Those who are seasoned patients maintain a sort of resignation: they know what will happen and it's familiar. New patients are clearly nervous— anxious to know what's in store. These unique levels of life experiences, in the moment, waft around us all. And for everyone, no matter what the role, the prayer is that this hideous cancer will be cured.

> Wow...what a perfect narrative of who you were, who you have become, and how you can impact and comfort others who have yet to travel down this road, simply with a smile and a welcoming spirit. Prayers are always with you, and now joy, peace, and a blessed feeling of accomplishment and hopeful anticipation can be added to those prayers! Hugs to you both as you get stronger and stronger daily. After all, you _are_ all about Strong Will!
> —Sally R

> Your words bring tears to my eyes and overwhelming love to my heart. So beautifully written and I can visualize the emotional and physical space as you describe it! Love you both!
> —Linda, Marcia's sister

> Your inspired descriptions help us to better understand what it is like for you and others facing cancer treatment. Sharing is a gift to all of us who read this and help us feel part of your journey. Hopefully you are feeling our prayers and love.
> —Diane

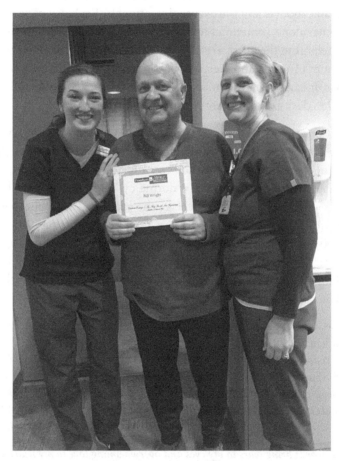

Bill and his super sweet technicians celebrate his last day of radiation

Stick a Fork in Me~ I'm Done!

April 27, 2018

Glorious words: Bill is done with radiation. Aaron surprised him arriving at the Cancer Center while he had his treatment today. We waited outside the area where patients get their treatment to watch and the technicians were so gracious about us being there. Four computer screens monitor the radiation process— if the one monitoring Bill's breathing senses anything irregular, all of the screens lock until it is rectified. It's an impressively managed system. Once he finished, Bill rang the big chime and everyone clapped. Finally, he met with Dr. Erickson, his radiation oncologist, who celebrated this accomplishment and sent us off with big hugs. The gratitude flows today!

> *Wow, that is the best news of the day! "It is finished!" Glad all went well. What a great feeling for both of you! Now go and enjoy the weekend!*
> *—Dianna*

> *Family is so important. So glad the radiation is complete.*
> *—Debbie*

> *TGIF has a whole new meaning for you guys, does it not? Excellent news and to have all of you there to ring the bells? Well it was just a perfect end, it seems.*
> *—Louann*

Family..... the Best

April 29, 2018

Both Zac and Aaron were with us this week end which was so lovely. For the non-sports followers, the NFL Draft was on TV absorbing their attention. Saturday, we had breakfast (including Bill who ate robustly) and went off to shop and explore while he power napped. I enjoyed it immensely! Sunday, the three of us went out again for brunch while Bill opted to stay home. Our collective time together was immensely pleasant and it's always great to have that young energy around us. Tonight was quiet. Liz, a new friend I've made here, brought Bill communion again which he really appreciated. These next days are for resting, rebuilding strength, and feeling relief from all the treatments. Sending peace to all.

> *The weekend is what you needed. Family is so important.*
>
> *—Ginny*

> *That sounds wonderful and peaceful.*
>
> *—Claudia*

> *It sounds like a wonderful weekend after all you've been through. I hope it's the first of many.*
>
> *—Sue*

> *Nice to have family visits! Hopefully, your weather is warming up some and you and Bill can sit or walk in some sunshine. It has warmed up a bit here but not as much as I think it should! My thoughts are with you and Bill for the next adventure.*
>
> *—Nancy H*

E-X-H-A-U-S-T-E-D

May 1, 2018

Bill says he's given his all to get to this point and he is just exhausted. He asked for a wheelchair today to get to appointments. We are at the Day Hospital where he had bloodwork and fluids. Blood pressure is very low (97/66) and his extremities ache. This means dehydration. Fluids will help immensely, so we are in the right place—again. While he sleeps and the fluids trickle, I'm thinking a rotisserie chicken will hit the spot tonight and give Bill some needed protein. Clean sheets are on the bed and hopefully this simple combo should help this guy begin to recoup energy and regain his "Strong Will."

P. S. The blood pressure is already back to normal. Bill is visiting with Aaron who stopped by so maybe we'll need more than rotisserie chicken for dinner.

> *He's been through WWIII... he deserves much rest before the next one. Love and strength to you both.*
> > *—Linda, Marcia's sister*

> *I love hearing from you every day. I know you are going through such a hard time right now so I pray for you as well as Bill.*
> > *—Luana*

> *Though we are neighbors, we live separate lives. Never ever feel alone because we are here in strength, thoughts and +prayers! At a time like this I remember the Footprint Prayer.*
> > *—Shannon*

> *I think of that prayer often (One of Bill's few responses in this journal.)*
> > *—William Wright*

> *Exhausted probably applies to both of you. I'm wishing you both much rest and good food to get stronger. Prayers that Bill regains some strength soon.*
> > *—Sue*

Conduit for Life

May 2, 2018

Many years ago, when my mother died, I talked to a colleague who said "Now you are a wounded healer." At first it didn't make sense— but as I thought about it, I realized this truth. Loss wounds us. We're never the same, but we can use what we've learned from that loss to help others to heal.

This cancer journey is a conduit for life— Bill's treatment, surgery, and recovery is the desired path— his conduit for life. But what we are learning is how *we* can be a conduit for others. Two people from home have contacted us to learn more about Dr. Evans' work with patients who have this same diagnosis. When you've walked this road you know the reality of tenuous hope for those who have little or none. To be a part of that in some minuscule way is overwhelming! It's a glorious privilege to think of this potential: to be a conduit for life, for hope, for others.

> *We all touch one another more than we know...everyone's individual experiences compound to powerfully lift and heal one another. God is the all-knowing caregiver that joins us all.*
>
> *—Jim and Carolyn, Bill's brother-in-law and sister*

> *Perfectly written. Empathy vs sympathy. Prayed this morning that Bill will gain a little more steam today. Always praying for Him to provide you with unimaginable strength. When you stay in line with His plan for you, He will always reward you with needed strength, energy and words for those around you, when there seem to be days with nothing left for you to give. Sounds like you found a great ray of understanding of at least one purpose of this journey! Keep looking! He has all kinds of pockets of joy all around you while you walk this out!*
>
> *—Sally R*

> *It's so inspiring how encouraging you can be. I am hoping and praying for energy and healing.*
>
> *—Cindy M*

Shhh, Don't Tell

May 3, 2018

(Read in a whisper) It's Thursday. Bill doesn't have any appointments. He doesn't have to be anywhere. He can stay home, relax, and let the last of the radiation do its job.

Now, use a normal voice— but read this elatedly because I will:

He said he's feeling *better* today! And, he's thinking a *walk* would be nice! And, he *enjoyed* a good breakfast! *And,* he ate half of a chicken sandwich for lunch, which is more food intake than we have seen in a long time.

Boom! Thank you, God, for answered prayers.

Easy Peasy

May 4, 2018

Today is a fluids day for Bill. There is an affiliated medical campus about five minutes from home— making this a very convenient place to rejuvenate and hydrate when there aren't doctor appointments. The week end is wide open and no one is more pleased about that than Bill.

> *Sounds good.*
>
> *—Ginny*

> *Enjoy your completely free weekend! Hope the sun is shining, the sky blue and the clouds fluffy white.*
>
> *—Marcia L*

> *Enjoy the time that is just all yours to do as you like and on your own time table! Must be nice to have a bit of more normal things to consider where and what you want to do.*
>
> *—Louann*

> *Peaceful!*
>
> *—Cindy H*

> *Enjoy your weekend! I hope you have some good weather.*
>
> *—Sue*

> *Have a fantastic and peace filled weekend.*
>
> *—Julie S*

Today's Winner

May 5, 2018

Bill and I both picked Justify as the winning horse in the Kentucky Derby—but that's the only winner today. After two days of feeling better, today was a step back for him. It is a wide open week end so he can take it easy and maybe tomorrow will be better.

> Good time to have a little set back if it has to be as the week is open and his body is not scheduled to be invaded by healing, yet, horrific at times, curative meds. Enjoy the time to do as you want on your own schedule.
> —Louann

> The up and downs of your journey. Hope tomorrow is a better day. Blessings.
> —Ginny

> Sorry to hear that, Marcia. Tomorrow will be a better day. Prayers and good thoughts for you both.
> —Julie J

> Hopes and prayers that tomorrow will be a day for Bill to be feeling better.
> —Sue

Unexpected Rewards

May 6, 2018

When you face a really serious illness, there are many aspects of fighting the disease that can consume you. Appointments, tests, treatment, and a whole lot of IV bags. Granted, it's not easy. Some days are discouraging and downright awful. Today we watched the movie based on the book, <u>The Shack</u>. It's the story of a man who questions his faith. God, Jesus, and the Holy Spirit are uniquely personified. I was eager to see what Bill thought of it and we had a good discussion about the main character's struggles. We saw ourselves in the main character in different ways. What is so special about these conversations is bringing them into the here and now of this fight we're in. We ask "why" and so did Mack, the main character. We argue. So did Mack. We judge. As did Mack. Using this movie as another lens for seeing God, His infinite love and wisdom, keeps shaping us as learners— or yearners— in our faith walk. It's just another way of running spiritual sandpaper over the roughness of our imperfect souls— all with the goal of smoothing us out, forgiving our sins, and making us worthy. I'm not sure we would have had this discussion *before* cancer. Now the stakes are higher— we seek to understand the plan He has for us. It's a cumbersome struggle but there is an unexpected beauty sharing it with someone you love deeply.

Great book! Always praying.

—Dody

Found the book riveting but it was several years ago so should get it out and have another go at it. Think each time one will get something different and yet relevant from it. Nice topic for you both to share at this time it seems.

—Louann

The book is a great read. So glad you saw the movie. Thinking of you both and praying for Bill's recovery.

—Dawn

I too loved this movie - even more than the book. I think the author would be thrilled with your response to it. You can't help but feel God's love in all three "persons." I found it very comforting. I hope you and Bill felt that too.

—Diane

Your post touched both Jim and me. We watched "The Shack" together when it first came out, and you would have thought we each watched a different movie as we started to react to it and discuss it. Jim, as you know, is an outdoor man: hunting, fishing, trapping, camping, canoeing, sailing and shooting skeet. He shared how many times and in how many ways God had reached him and taught him through His creation of earth and its beauty. He learned how to let go and let God. I saw it in a much different way as a teacher trying to find a way to reach struggling students who were often hurt and angry. As we talked, we learned so much about each other. Thank you for sharing this post today. It brought back a precious time together for this old married couple.

—Linda S

Late Night Field Trip

May 7, 2018

It's late Monday and we are at the Center for Advanced Care, a specialized ER for cancer patients. This 24 Hour Clinic opened about a year ago and other hospitals are looking at this model because it's so helpful when there are urgent needs for cancer patients. They aren't exposed to germs from the general population. Bill is having shortness of breath, feeling light headed and blacking out. He had fluids today and that usually gets him back on track, but not tonight. They are running tests to see what might be triggering this. He is under the care of two nurses and a nurse practitioner who are consulting with the doctors. So, those of you who are reading Caring Bridge© at this late hour, please say a prayer as you close your eyes tonight.

> *They are on their way to all of you. It is wonderful to have such a resource you can access quickly and easily without fear of picking up more germs. Still, frightening to say the least.*
>
> *—Louann*

> *More prayers for more healing. He is present.*
>
> *—Jim, Bill's brother-in-law*

> *Big healing thoughts coming Bill's way. Hugs to you, Marcia!*
>
> *—Nancy H*

Serious News

May 8, 2018

Bill has extensive blood clots in his lungs. He's being admitted for several days for treatment. We're so glad they urged us to come in and get checked. As we know more, I'll share. Please keep Bill in your prayers.

> *Prayers from Barcelona. I'm thinking of you two. I'd sounds like you're in the right place, though.*
>
> *—Barbara*

> *Wow. Not what you want to learn but the miracle is that you are right there and dealing with the top tier in the field. So glad you made this decision to go and be treated by this specific group. Know Bill is in the best possible hands— but please make sure to take care of you. In many ways this is probably way harder on you.*
>
> *—Louann*

> *Oh my. So very grateful that Bill is getting care for the clot. Thankful you are where you need to be. So stressful for you, Marcia. Know that support, love and prayers are with you both.*
>
> *—Julie S*

> *Jesus....right now— we need you! Invade Bill and remove the blood clot. You are able and we come to you and ask you to intervene as only you can. We ask all of this in Your mighty name. Amen.*
>
> *—Sally R*

> *Prayers!*
>
> *—Ginny Weeks*

> *We pray for your family.*
>
> *—Jim, Bill's brother-in-law*

The Sun is Up

May 8, 2018

It's dawn in Milwaukee. Clots in *both* lungs are unusual but lung clots, in general, are a common side effect for pancreatic cancer. He's receiving Heparin and magnesium. A team of thoracic surgeons will be coming in shortly to evaluate the possibility of surgery. He hasn't slept much, but I'm pretty sure I nodded off for a couple hours. Keep the prayers coming, dear friends. More as soon as we know.

> *Jesus, we come again for Your touch right now, Jesus, Bill needs your touch. We have put our faith in you and call on that now. Please allow Bill to be your miracle, a testimony of your strength and healing power. Right now Jesus, right now.*
>
> *—Sally R*

> *Lord, wrap your arms around Bill and Marcia. Give them your peace. Send healing to Bill, and give his doctors wisdom and guidance to know exactly what Bill needs at this time.*
>
> *—Linda L*

> *Storming the heavens! May the God of all being be powerfully with you on this latest step of your journey. Lots of love.*
>
> *—Pat S*

> *Again, exactly the right place with the experienced doctors right there to determine the best course of action as he continues on this journey with you right by his side. Thanks so much for taking your precious time to let us all know what is going on. Another task for you but so many of us are so very grateful you are putting time and energy into this site.*
>
> *—Louann*

Resting Comfortably

May 8, 2018

Bill is settled into his room and feeling a bit better tonight. Aaron is here which always cheers him up. His ultimate treatment hasn't been finalized but we'll know more tomorrow. Doctors are pleased that he's responding to the IV medications and all other preliminary tests are coming back favorably. Dr. Evans is attending a medical conference but sent three of the doctors who train with him to check on Bill. It's reassuring to know he's being followed so carefully. So for tonight, we all should sleep well.

> *Praying that you all rest comfortably and peacefully tonight.*
> *—Diane*

> *Thanks for the update. Hope all get a good night's rest. Continuing prayers.*
> *—Ginny*

> *Good to hear Bill is comfortable and responding to meds. May you rest too, friend.*
> *—Julie S*

> *So happy to hear Bill is responding well to his latest issue Marcia. Bless you both and prayers are continuing for both of you.*
> *—Julie J*

> *Hope the rising sun this morning brings faith and hope.*
> *—Cindy H*

Tonight's Epilogue

May 8, 2018

No sooner did I publish the last update but the door opened and in walked Bill's surgeon, Dr. Evans. He'd been out of town, flew home, and stopped at the hospital to see Bill! One of his concerns is that he wants his lungs strong and healthy for surgery. He will check Bill's films tomorrow along with his progress. He is a gifted and compassionate doctor and as you all know, the reason we're here. Aaron finally got to meet him and as they shook hands, I noticed he was wearing the purple "Strong Will" bracelet* we gave him. Now that's a very caring detail.

(*see cover of the book)

Dr. Evans and your caregivers are a gift from the Lord. His goodness is present even in the most difficult times.

—Jim, Bill's brother-in-law

My assumption is that he is getting as much from you as you from him. While it is your struggle, he is along and the guide for it, so that all of you are a team and have confidence in one another. Seems in so many ways you were all meant to be in this together. Know you are all happy he is back and right on board with the treatment plan. Anxious for tomorrow's news after he sees the films and the changes that have happened since he has been on the drugs.

—Louann

Dr. Evans must be very compassionate. Besides skill, compassion has to be the most important attribute of a physician. Prayers that Bill will have a good day of healing.

—Sue

O is for Oxygen

May 9, 2018

There was some discussion about sending Bill home with oxygen tomorrow (at least we *think* tomorrow) but he did well walking with the occupational therapist (who is coincidentally from Ann Arbor, Michigan— about thirty miles from our home) so it's not necessary. He's responding to the medication and his heart got an A+ from all tests. He says he's feeling good so things are looking better at the hospital today. My sister, Linda is here and we spent time visiting with him but left for a while so he could sleep. Aaron met us for lunch which was delightful and the day seems to be moving in the right directions.

> *Been waiting all day to get the update and it is so worth it. Miracles are happening all the time it seems and it is just wonderful for all involved. I must say he seems to respond quickly when they get the right stuff in him. Yippee!*
>
> *—Louann*

> *This is great news! Keeping you in our prayers. Love you guys!*
>
> *—Cindy M*

> *We love you guys, too.*
>
> *—William Wright, another response from Bill*

> *Such good news. You must all be over the moon.*
>
> *—Julie J*

> *I think God is up there sometimes saying "Do you need a little boost to know I'm right here with you today?*
> *BING! There you go!" And now joy comes in the morning of a brand new day for healing and restoration! Heal on!*
>
> *—Sally R*

Discharge

May 10, 2018

Bill called early this morning before we headed to the hospital to tell me he's being discharged this afternoon. Linda is here with me and we will leave soon to bring him home. He had a little chest pain when he walked briskly but that's the clot "fussing" and it will get better they are saying. It's sunny and lovely in Milwaukee this morning— a good harbinger for the events of the day.

> *A phone call like no other I know. Can see the smiles on both faces and hear the excitement in his voice. By sundown he will be right where he needs to be, with you and family in his own home and own bed and surroundings. We all know the joy of that!*
>
> *—Louann*

> *I'm so glad that Bill will be able to come home. Resting at home is so much easier.*
>
> *—Sue R*

> *Great news. Celebrate in the beauty of the day and the goodness of God! I think it is the Gerard Manley Hopkins poem that starts "Glory be to God for dappled things." Enjoy that kind of day. Lots of love, and both begging prayers and prayers of thanksgiving continue.*
>
> *—Pat S*

> *Prayers were answered!*
>
> *—Cherryl*

Not So Fast...

May 10, 2018

Well, maybe discharge is on hold. Medical staff wants to make certain Bill's heart is OK since he had discomfort on exertion. Updates as they come.

> *It really does not matter as it is on the table— and the last thing you need is to get home and have to return. Get it all tuned up and running while in the "shop" and remember these words are from a born and bred Badger!*
>
> *—Louann*

> *It's better to make sure that the heart is okay. Hopefully he'll be able to go home soon.*
>
> *—Ginny*

> *In a great place right now to get the help he needs. Stay strong in your faith. Prayers continue.*
>
> *—Julie J*

> *Better safe than sorry comes to mind. The medical staff seems so very conscientious.*
>
> *—Sue*

Tentative Discharge

May 10, 2018

The word tonight: collect more data on Bill's heart and providing all is well— he will be discharged tomorrow. Discomfort is attributed to the clots and not further heart problems, yet they want to be certain before sending him home. Grateful for all the prayers and well wishes.

> *Well, OK, then. Let's see what Friday brings.*
>
> *- Louann*

> *Better safe than sorry. Continued prayers and hopes that he can be discharged.*
>
> *-Ginny*

Will I Stay or Will I Go?

May 11, 2018

Discharge is still up in the air. Bill is very dehydrated with a big deficit in fluid intake so he's getting more— and more IV bags of rejuvenating fluids. His blood pressure has been very low and now it's registering in the normal range. I'll pause this journal and finish when we have the verdict.....

****

He's discharged!!! Heading home.

> *Eureka...a true gift. Have a nice relaxing time this weekend and both of you keep the fluids flowing, yours of a different type, Marcia, for obvious reasons. Again, thanks so much for taking the time to keep all of us up to date.*
>
> *—Louann*

> *No place like home! Praying for a special weekend for truly special people.......Blessings.....*
>
> *—Sally P*

> *Cha Ching!!!!! So glad that he is able to go home. Just rest and relax and enjoy!!!!*
>
> *—Dawn*

> *Ahhhhhh. Relax.*
>
> *—Cindy H*

> *Nice! Hope you get lots of rest and only good news for Bill's surgery. Thanks for all the updates! Hugs to you and Bill.*
>
> *—Nancy*

> *So much more restful for both of you at home.*
>
> *—Debbie*

There's No Place Like Home

May 11, 2018

Dorothy may have said it best, but Bill is feeling the beloved phrase "There's no place like home." He had a light dinner, a soaking bath, and eased into bed. He's sleeping soundly and hopefully without pain. It's so good to have him home with meds to help him recover and time to do just that. Thank you all.

> *You get right into bed, too, so you can stay rested at this time.*
>> —*Louann*

> *Wonderful!! Take care.*
>> —*Cherryl*

> *Good news! Now about you getting much needed rest?*
>> —*Luana*

That Was The Week That Was

May 13, 2018

It's good to turn the corner on a new week with last week's issues wearing so deeply on Bill. We spent a quiet weekend home. Aaron and his mom, visiting from Michigan, stopped to see us Saturday. Zac came later that evening and stayed overnight to celebrate Mother's Day with me before heading back to Chicago. It was just the right amount of time with company. Bill slept some Saturday evening and Sunday morning but was up and enjoyed dinner with us Sunday afternoon. This week he will meet with endocrinology and get fluids Monday, Wednesday, and Friday. Restorative time is in order for a man rebuilding his strength.

> Bill and Marcia, sending a little sunshine, to sprinkle in your days, reminding you that you're thought of, in a warm and special way! Continued prayers from myself and our church family. Hoping for a very positive week ahead! Thank you for all the updates. I read them as they come on the Caring Bridge© site. What a powerful tool someone created for all of us to stay in touch. God Bless you both!
>
> —Dianna

> Such a good report. I'm not a big Willy Nelson fan, but his song "You Were Always On My Mind" seems to fit us right now. Maybe we don't post a comment every day, but, we do pray for you every day, and we read your posts every day, and You Are Always On Our Minds, dear friends. We have learned so much by sharing your journey. Sending love and smiles today for your peaceful weekend.
>
> —Linda S

> God put just enough "family" into your weekend to refuel and refresh you... even though it wears to be "on" for Bill. Could not be more pleased to know this week is one for you to both gain some strength! Lean into your Master Healer, and remember this song: It's such a powerful reminder that our God is working "in the waiting." Love and hugs for a great week!
>
> —Sally R

I'm Beginning to See It!

May 14, 2018

After Bill's fluid infusion today, we met with endocrinology about nutrition post-surgery. Since he's likely to have surgically induced diabetes, we learned about changes and adjustments that will be in order if that is the case. We both felt the meeting was disorganized. The dietician was flighty and couldn't retain information we shared with her. She had an intern and at one point, even the intern seemed overwhelmed by the dietician's demeanor. It was almost comical and we left hoping that will be revisited down the road—hopefully with different staff. However, the big takeaway for me today is that even though Bill is still very, very tired, I'm seeing more normalcy in him. Tonight he really enjoyed dinner. I made banana bread, which hit the spot. It's incremental, but for all he's been through, nurse Marcia sees him turning the corner and she's so proud and thrilled to see that!

> So glad to hear Bill was feeling better. Even the "little" things that are improving are huge steps. Keep baking that "banana bread!" You are in my prayers daily. Hugs!
>
> —Cherryl

> Great news about things tasting good again. Too bad about the flighty nutritionist and intern. It will be better next time and you will have a different set of ears listening to you and offering some useful information.
>
> —Louann

> And surely he has the best nurse in the world and knows it!
>
> —Amy, Marcia's sister

Things Are On The Move

May 15, 2018

The CT scan scheduled for two weeks from now is happening much sooner. It will be next Monday with follow up with Dr. Evans on Tuesday. The significance is that:

a) we will know how the tumor responded to chemo and radiation and
b) depending on how Bill's lungs are healing, we may have a new surgery date *or* stick with the original date of June 4th.

It's a very pivotal time and seems like it's been a long time coming, but now it's very close! Bill had another good day feeling stronger and able to enjoy meals again in moderation. All positive progress. Now if only his iPhone hadn't died. An Apple Store field trip is on the docket for tomorrow.

> *We so appreciate your daily updates. These days are very precious and it's wonderful Bill is making progress. Here's hoping next week's appointment provides very encouraging news.*
>
> *—Margaret*

> *Wow, exciting news! Whether the surgery date is moved up or not, how wonderful he is feeling better. Hope and wish that all news is positive! Have fun at the Apple store. They are always responsive and it is usually a quick in and out.*
>
> *—Nancy H*

> *Love to hear Bill is feeling better. Take care and prayers.*
>
> *—Cherryl*

> *I'm so glad that Bill is feeling a little bit on the mend. I hope the Apple Store outing is successful!*
>
> *—Sue*

Dave and Bill

A Joyful Reunion

May 16, 2018

Bill's very dear friend, Dave, flew here from Florida to see him. It's only a short visit but that's good for Bill right now as he gets stronger. His wife, Kathy, also a dear friend, couldn't come this time but we posted her photo at the dinner table to simulate her presence and had a good chuckle over that. Bill seems perkier every day and seeing Dave added to his happiness. We had some great "catch up" conversation followed by lasagna for dinner which Bill requested and enjoyed! Tomorrow is a "no appointment day" and that is so nice to anticipate. Since I managed to break a tooth a couple days ago, I'm going to the dentist. I guess we just *have* to have something on the calendar.

> *A day full of normal— what a blessing! And a visitor, too. May the perk level keep rising.*
> *Prayers from home! Lots and lots of them.*
>
> —*Julie S*

> *More good news. Seeing a good friend is medicine in a way. Sorry you have a tooth problem. Prayers.*
>
> —*Ginny*

> *Oh dear, about the tooth— but good you were able to find a local dentist to take care of it. The rest of the note is just starting to sound more normal with visits and favorite meals and a wide open day minus your "chore." It sounds good and must feel good to all of you. Next update will have info on how the tooth event went and how you guys can now laugh about some of the catching up tales you two shared with Dave. Sounds good.*
>
> —*Louann*

It's a Beautiful Day in the Neighborhood

May 17, 2018

What a joy it is to have little health reporting to do today! Bill and Dave tackled the Apple Store with no resolution— but tomorrow he will go back after having tried some tips they suggested to try at home. We think the phone may be shot and a new phone is on the horizon; but it's lovely to grumble about ordinary things and enjoy a beautiful sunny spring day in Wisconsin. Aaron joined us for dinner and it was, as always, lovely to be together. Dave heads back to his beloved Kathy and Florida tomorrow. It's been wonderful to have him here. So as we wrap up this simple day, we are contented. I have a new crown—for my tooth— not to be confused with royalty.

> *So glad you got your crown. If that wasn't going to work, would they have given you a "Caring Bridge?" (Just couldn't resist).*
>
> *—Linda S*

> *Happy to hear you enjoyed some ordinary grumblings-love it! Prayers for continued ordinary days and building strength.*
>
> *—Julie S*

> *Ahh! For what most would consider mundane—hugs.*
>
> *—Cindy H*

> *What a nice way to start a weekend. Ordinary days are wonderful! Prayers continue. Hugs!*
>
> *—Cherryl*

> *How wonderful to rejoice in the simple blessing of ordinary! Something all of us should remember.*
>
> *—Marcia L*

> *I'm sorry you have ordinary crummy things to worry about like teeth and phones, but glad it's not the big stuff. Prayers that soon you and Bill only have ordinary things to worry about.*
>
> *—Sue*

Little Ones Make Big Smiles

May 19, 2018

Aaron's good friend, Justin, brought his adorable four year old to visit and see Bill today. We had hot dogs and chips because little Harrison *loves* hot dogs. Bill had a turkey sandwich but thoroughly enjoyed the visit and enthusiasm of Justin's son. They spent a couple of hours here and when they left, Bill took a nap. The stimulation and the activity wore him out. Earlier today, Bill used some weights and got a little exercise but regaining normal levels of energy will take time.

> *Simple things can be refreshing and little people and hot dogs would be on that list for sure. I hope he knows that having the interest in even trying the weights is spectacular. Pretty sure I would find reasons not to do the very things that are necessary on the road to recovery. Bravo for all of you!*
> —Louann

> *"Little ones" do wonders to help you enjoy your day! Glad to hear you are having a nice weekend! Take care.*
> —Cherryl

> *A child can do wonders. Sounds like there's more normalcy each day. Good news.*
> —Ginny

> *Yeah, for hot dogs and kiddoes!*
> —Cindy H

Heartbreaking News

May 22, 2018

Today we learned cancer has spread to Bill's liver which means no surgery. We've known since Sunday this was likely because Bill was in the emergency room late Saturday night with severe pain and had a CT scan of the liver. Dr. Evans confirmed it today. It was so helpful to have our boys with us at the appointment to support us.

Bill wants to fight on. There is a new chemotherapy that may stall and even kill these hideous cells. We see the oncologist here tomorrow and will set a new direction. I'm so proud of my precious Bill for his strength and tenacity. The PA who works with Dr. Evans hugged Bill as we left and whispered to him, "You have a wonderful attitude!" Indeed he does.

While we don't know the schedule as such yet, we believe we will stay here for two more months. Healthcare is so much closer than driving to Beaumont Hospital in Michigan and we have the critical care unit available 24 hours. This is so awful for us to absorb. We had such hopes for the surgery and ultimate healing/cure. Now we are trying to buy time, sustain quality of life, and praying fervently for that miracle.

> *Our hearts ache for you and tears flow freely. It won't stop our prayers for you both as you face new choices and decisions. We continue our love and support. I wish we were close enough in proximity to give hugs and physical comfort and help to dry your tears.*
>
> *—Linda S*

> *So sorry to hear this news, I pray for Bill that he continues to have the strength to keep on trying for new cures and better days ahead. I also pray for you Marcia as you support your husband by being cheerful and keeping everything together. Give each other hugs often and never give up hope for the miracle, no matter what that may be. God bless you both!*
>
> *—Pam L*

What can be said except what the others have written? Prayers for all of you and the hope for a plan that will provide the best care and course of treatment that is available. Sounds like being there is, again, the ray of hope. So happy you have the facility and staff that you have grown close to. They have obviously taken you into their lives. Must have been so hard to write this, but thank you for keeping us in the loop.

—Louann

I am so sorry to hear of this setback. I join everyone else here in fervent prayer for Bill's healing and complete recovery. I know God hears us. I know Bill is special to God. With love and trust and hope, I am praying for you and your family with all of my strength and faith.

—Lynne

Now What?

May 24, 2018

After meeting with the oncologist here yesterday, Bill decided to have the new class of chemotherapy drugs to see if it will contain growth and spread of tumors. He will start next Wednesday and have it every other week for a two hour infusion. We are told patients handle this type well— it's less tough on the body but it will be vital to watch his blood levels closely as he goes through this treatment with so much previous chemo and radiation. We can only hope it is a course that his body tolerates well and the tumors do not.

> *Wow, so glad you get choices quickly and can stay right where you are with a team that you know and that knows you. Hoping his body will continue to tolerate this intervention to provide the maximum benefit with the least side effects.*
>
> *—Louann*

> *Prayers this chemo will be a "magic bullet" so to speak. Bill's strength of will (and yours) to beat this awful disease is amazing.*
>
> *—Sue*

> *At least the journey has another direction and hope it does what it is supposed to. Continued prayers.*
>
> *—Ginny*

And Here We Are

May 25, 2018

Yesterday was the one year anniversary of Bill's heart stent placement. He "graduated" from the post procedure blood thinners, but so many other factors have arisen. Now he is on twice a day injections for the blood clots that *are* dissipating. The irony! He saw the cardiologist, as follow up to his hospital stay, who took him off blood pressure meds. It does seems nice to see *less* medications on the list. Everything checked out nicely in that department. Now he's getting fluids at the Day Hospital and we hope that will keep his hydration replenished. We've had so much to talk about with the new diagnosis. Days are numbing, scary, filled with tears, but we're striving hard to find joy in every day together and as Bill says, "just treasure breathing the same air."

Amazing how you can both see the good in such a topsy turvy time of your lives. Nice to see some let up in pills as that can be a positive topic in your talks that are centering on the latest not so good topic. My thoughts are with you and many cyber hugs heading west to your world.

—Louann

Louann's posts mirror my thoughts but she says things so eloquently that there is little left for me to say other than I miss you and pray every day for you and Bill and his team of care givers. It sounds like you could not be in better hands - Bill for his physical needs and you for your emotional ones. I watch for your posts every day and you are always so positive that when I see them I feel better from seeing your positive thoughts and comments. God be with you now and always.

—Luana

My heart is with you both. Thank you for sharing this journey with us, it helps to know how to pray. There is real blessing in that Bill is out one year from his heart issues. Cherish each and every moment, smile, hugs and family visits. I continue to pray for healing and comfort as you let God do his will.

—Pam L

Prayers for strength and comfort as God walks with you during this time. Your love for each other is such a treasure, and each day a new jewel. Peace be with you— my prayers continue.

—Valerie

I'm so sorry that your troubles have been mounting one on top of the other. Prayers for a peaceful, relaxing Memorial Day weekend. As scary and awful as a liver cancer diagnosis is, there have been tremendous strides in the last few years with newer drugs shrinking tumors and keeping them at bay. Prayers for some good healing to surround Bill.

—Sue

Nothing can be said that hasn't already been said. So I will say this—it seems as though you two were blessed to have each other. The strength and conviction you both have is inspiring. God bless you both- remember who's carrying you.

—Shannon

Many meaningful, heartfelt comments. Love and prayers surround you. Your faithful daily blogs keep us in touch with each step of your journey. May your weekend be calm, enjoying each other " breathing the same air"

—Marcia L

A Peek at Milwaukee

May 26, 2018

My sister, Linda, came to see us yesterday and stayed through this afternoon. She's always a joy— upbeat, positive, and compassionate. This morning Bill, Linda and I took a short drive through town but Bill felt tackling the art museum was too much for him and sent the two of us off to explore it. The structure is beautiful and unique— right on Lake Michigan. It was hot and sunny so people were out and about enjoying the summer temps. We wandered in the museum and had lunch in the cafe overlooking the water. It was lovely and satisfied my curiosity about the place. Bill wants to go now so I'm hoping to go back soon.

> *It sounds like a very unique place, and it's a wonderful change of pace from medical venues. Hopefully, Bill will feel up to going one day soon.*
>
> *—Sue*

> *I've also visited this museum. The structure is amazing. How fortunate you are to have your sister close. So glad you had a pleasant day.*
>
> *—Margaret*

> *A break that you really needed. Hoping Bill will be up to going soon.*
>
> *—Linda L*

> *Nice break for you. Hope Bill will be up to going soon. At least he got out.*
>
> *—Ginny*

> *Hooray for sisters!*
>
> *—Debbie*

Carrying the Weight

May 27, 2018

Along the way we're bound to be hit with discouragement— especially when we've ridden the wave of high hopes for so long. The crash of last week's news has hit us both hard. We try to perk each other up but sometimes we both feel down at the same time. So we talk, we pray, we read hopeful texts— scripture, some wonderful books from my friend Sally. It helps numb things for a bit— anesthesia for the soul. But when you've had "it"-I mean the love we share- you dread a potential change. I pray there is a miracle yet to be granted and I hope it *is* God's will, but if it isn't, well, I have some mighty work to do to understand that. (I don't mean to offend my stalwart friends who have greater faith.) Having a place for my words and thoughts helps me. We are in a community where we know very few people and the Caring Bridge© website connects us to those of you who follow and support us. So on this Memorial Day weekend where heat has finally arrived amid the sunshine and lush green, I'll pause to breathe in the majesty of God's creation seeking fervently to be lifted up by His power and might.

> *The Lord is guiding you both through this difficult time. He will never give you more challenges than you can handle and He is always there to strengthen you. Who knows - maybe you have crossed paths with someone and you helped their faith. Prayers continue. Hugs!!*
>
> —Cherryl

> *As I read your daily thoughts I am constantly amazed at the strength of your faith and character. I don't believe God is "doing this" to you and Bill, but I do know He is with you through this painful time. Just as he has always been. I pray that you can feel his presence and love and that will carry both of you. You and Bill are in my prayers.*
>
> —Diane

Enough About Me

May 28, 2018

After yesterday's posting I'm committed to making today more about Bill, my hero. We are at the Day Hospital and Bill is getting fluids for hydration and overall comfort. There are many more patients here today than we expected since it's a holiday, but cancer doesn't take breaks. It's oddly comforting being here. It's probably the familiarity of this place. Over the last several months we've spent most of our time here for treatment, appointments, tests and labs. It's funny how that sequence builds a macabre sort of stability.

Again, right where you need to be that only those going thru a similar experience can truly understand. It is not even words just your common connection that forges a bond so very strong. So glad you are there and he is getting what he needs, fluids, rest, comfort and wonderful Y-O-U leading us in the cheering section.

—Louann

I love to read Louann's posts. She expresses herself so beautifully and one can sense the depth of your friendship and the strength of her support!

—Marcia L

Your post yesterday really touched my heart. You trusted us with your feelings and we all understood your honesty and how hard it is to share your doubts and fears. That took great courage, friend. Thank you for that. It isn't just about Bill. It isn't just about you. It is about this journey you are taking together. We are privileged to share it with you, but we all understand that the highs and lows for us, are much higher and lower for the two of you. We don't forget or underestimate that. It makes us pray harder and love stronger.

—Linda S

I'm so glad Bill is getting his fluids. Most of us take fluids for granted. Also glad that the day hospital has become a place where you both know he can get the treatment he needs to be comfortable. Your posting yesterday was very honest and real. It's got to be very scary to be set adrift in the unknown sea that is cancer. I'm sure that many more prayers were lifted up for the two of you.

—Sue

Steak and (a little) "Shaken"

May 29, 2018

Bill has wanted a filet ever since we've been in Wisconsin but anytime we made a reservation at a restaurant, his digestive track rebelled so we cancelled. Tonight we found the perfect alternative. We brought filets home and Aaron joined us. He found a great method for grilling without a grill using the stove top and oven. It worked perfectly. Fresh asparagus and a small plain baked potato delighted Bill (and us). We watched a little of the Milwaukee Brewers game on TV and a guest in the press box was Dr. Evans! A trainer for the team is a patient who *did* have the lifesaving pancreatic surgery so the two of them were interviewed. We felt so sad knowing we aren't in that circle of hope any longer. It's wonderful to know this man is, but we were a bit shaken to see this tonight— just wish it could be Bill, too.

Oh how we all wish it were Bill. I think about you both and would love to have a magic wand. Praying for a miracle.

—Dawn

Amazingly small world, is it not sometimes? Glad you were able to figure out how to have a meal that he has been thinking about for some time. Sounds pretty good to me also. And the Brewers? Well, please do not give up on our Tigers! Going to the game Saturday here. Keep on keeping on and maybe repeat the meal as needed....

—Louann

Ouch! That is a painfully small world!
Only God knows what lies ahead for any one of us. You all continue to be held in my prayers daily.

—Claudia

Your circle of hope is now different....... praying for the miracle to make all the differences. So glad God worked to have Aaron there.

—Cindy H

Back in the Saddle

May 30, 2018

After bloodwork and a consult with the oncologist, Bill started a new course of chemo today. Side effects that plagued him in the previous chemo aren't part of this regimen but this class of chemo has *different* potential side effects. So we'll cross our fingers and pray that Bill responds favorably. It will be one day a week every other week for three months with CT scans to assess progress after that period of time. This may alter our return to Michigan but with "weeks off," Bill may feel like a short road trip and it might just be to the Great Lakes state. We hear summer is beautiful there.

> *Hoping and praying that the different side effects are less brutal. The idea of maybe a short trip home must have lots of appeal to see your own house and all that is familiar. Time will tell but you continue to be in my thoughts and prayers daily.*
>
> —*Louann*

> *Oh, I hope and pray for good results with the new chemo! There is "no place like home."*
>
> —*Dawn*

> *Prayers that this chemo will go really well with minimal side effects. Bill deserves to have something go well. So far, summer has been highly overrated here. First it was too cold and wet and now too hot, humid and wet.*
>
> —*Sue*

A Not So Down Day

May 31, 2018

It's a no appointment, down day, day off from everything. Bill was promised this type of chemo won't be too hard on him and so far so good. His appetite is good. He's close to a clean bathroom, has great air conditioning, and that's a good foundation as he naps to rejuvenate his stamina. His mom, two brothers, and sister-in-law are coming to see him this week end and anticipating that amount of company requires him to front load with extra rest. Hopefully everyone will understand short visits are best for him and if he needs to sleep he can. There's a peace about us today as we enter this phase of new chemo. Feeling around for miracles. Maybe they're not too far away.

> *Claiming any and all small miracles that show up all through your days! Enjoy the "deep breath" time, and use it to find time to reconnect to His power, grace and unending love for you and Bill. He has been the same God that is crazy, madly in love with you yesterday, today and forever in your future!*
>
> *—Sally R*

> *Praying for miracles, rest, healing and cherished family visits.*
>
> *—Pam P*

> *So glad to hear the new chemo may be not as hard on Bill. Enjoy your weekend with family and friends— that is always good medicine!! Prayers continue for you both. Take care!!*
>
> *—Cherryl*

> *I like that you tell us about all kinds of days: the good, the bad and the ugly. That means a lot.*
>
> *—Linda S*

> *Sending good karma for days ahead and thankful for any and all good moments you both can have...including rest.*
>
> *—Linda, Marcia's sister*

Aligning with Hope

June 1, 2018

Bill got fluids at the day hospital today and as we waited for the hydration to do its work, Bill remarked that despite his feeling discouraged, the setting was soothing. He had a private room with a bed and recliner and semi-private bath. There is a reassurance that comes with the familiarity of this routine. He's also discovered some of his regular supplements seem to be adding to his digestion in a not so positive way and eliminating them may be a real game changer for him in terms of comfort and predictability. Some of these small factors can make a big difference going forward. And, while all this unfolds unremarkably, I'm feeling hopeful. Uplifted. Miracles *do* happen and I'm not so sure we will be "passed over." Believing in the unseen is one of the biggest challenges we face as Christians—so I'm aligning my faith with hope and working on believing in the unseen.

> *Amen!*
>
> *—Sally P*

> *Two words.........AMEN and AMEN!*
>
> *—Sally R*

> *I can't even imagine the roller coaster of emotions you must face each day. Continued prayers for exactly what you need by the Creator of miracles.*
> *—Debbie L*

> *I will echo the Amen comments...and also say you are an inspiration to me. Your faith and your courage are amazing!*
> *—Marcia L*

> *The Great Physician has Bill in his arms!! Many prayers continue for you both—with love!!*
> *—Nancy B*

**Bill and his brothers, Sam and Tom with their mother,
Rita (age 93) visit us in Wisconsin**

A Very Special Day

June 2, 2018

Life can get so busy that time passes and we miss connecting to people who are our "kin." Today was very special because Bill's two brothers, Sam and Tom, sister-in-law Cathy, and Bill's mom all came to see him. It was good to be together and Bill really enjoyed it. He was up the entire day laughing and joking and being present in the togetherness. Aaron and friend Zach from Michigan arrived in the late afternoon so all the guys had a beer at the local bar two blocks from us. It's moments like these we treasure, snap a mental picture to capture it, and sit back to simply savor.

> *Bill, what a great pic of friends and family. Love your big smile!*
>
> *—Nancy H*

> *What a lovely day. Bill looks so happy. Nothing better than family to lift your spirits.*
>
> *—Diane*

> *Three cheers and Thanks be for a "normal" kick back and relax day. As healing as love and prayers. A 3D version of that!*
>
> *—Pat*

> *Glad today was a good day. I look forward to your posts every day and they always have something positive- even if the day wasn't the best. Makes me feel humble when I complain about something in my day.*
>
> *—Luana*

The Practice of Gratitude

June 3, 2018

Dr. Brené Brown has a podcast called, "Daring Greatly". Our niece Mackenzie sent it to both of us and it's well worth a listen. For me, I couch it in the present. When she talks about gratitude as a practice, it really resonates. We certainly have things *not* to be grateful for, but far more to *be* grateful for (please excuse those dangling prepositions). We can see any interface or life experience as just that—life. But when we dig in for a piece of gratitude, it's so much richer. Our weekend with Bill's family was so special. I'm grateful they made the trip to see him and so glad the brothers had their time to talk, to joke, and be a little serious. It offered some much needed togetherness time for them. I'm grateful Bill felt the best he has in a long time. Aaron's good friend, Zach, spent the weekend in Milwaukee and the two young men stopped to see everyone again this morning as Zach left town. I'm grateful for those connections to young and vibrant lives. Tonight Bill is tuckered out and napping—but I'm grateful he can rest and regain his strength. It's not a very complicated or informative post today, but it's one of gratitude and it's *amazing* how good it feels to celebrate just that. I'm so grateful.

> Your "attitude of gratitude" today is very humbling to us. You see and create beauty in so many ways just by being yourself and sharing your honest feelings. Today you are our teacher. Thank you.
>
> —Linda S

> It's always wonderful when someone expounds on the benefits of gratitude! We all are blessed by it and all can usually, be more grateful! Thank you for sharing your hard earned wisdom.
>
> —Claudia

Cancelled

June 4, 2018

It's a basic word. Events are cancelled. Dates are cancelled. Appointments are cancelled. June 4th was a day of hope for us. Bill's surgery would have been today, and as we all know, it was cancelled because the latest CT scan revealed the cancer has spread. He's valiantly undergoing more chemo to hold off that hideous enemy but it's a tough day for him. We sought another opinion from Mayo Clinic and they called this morning stating what we expected— they don't have any other options for him. *Boom.* All these doors have closed and we seek to learn from this. Yes, we are grateful for this chance— even though it hasn't been the outcome we desired. We have met so many wonderful people and the care has been exceptional. Our Caring Bridge© supporters continue to offer hopeful and endearing words for which we are *beyond* grateful. But what are we to learn? Every life experience contributes to who we are—layer upon layer— over time. We armor up and take what comes. Some battles seem fruitless which is where Bill is today. It *is* discouraging. Answers aren't there right now. I cling to hope and pray for miracles that do happen. Will one be ours? We wait.

I know this is tough but I see one miracle and that is that you found one another and have had time to know true love and happiness and commitment. Not in the way you both imagined but to be there for one another during a time like this is nothing short of divine intervention. Know it does not help with the news you got but there are all of us in your corner.
—Louann

Such frustration! Yes, there are miracles but maybe a miracle isn't needed. Continue to hope for the new chemo to work. Hope Bill can also get plenty of rest, have a hearty appetite and keep fighting this terrible sickness. Positive thoughts of healing continue to stream your way.
—Nancy H

None of us know what the next minute, hour, or day will bring. May the new chemo be an answer to this terrible disease. Keep the faith and our prayers continue.
—Ginny

You have been so honest with your feelings: today the feeling is discouragement. It's okay and we share it with you. Waiting is often the hardest thing to do. It seems like waiting isn't doing anything; but it can be a time to renew your strength, and catch your breath. That is what we are praying for you both today. A brief time of respite and rest.

—Linda S

This is something no one wants to hear - ever. I am praying for a miracle for Bill. I was reading and found this quote - "God doesn't give us what we can handle. He helps us handle what we are given." You are walking through deep waters. I am praying for your strength and for a miracle for your Bill.

—Dawn

Turbulence

June 6, 2018

Victor Frankl said "Human freedom is choosing one's attitude in any given set of circumstances." These wise words, posted in large script on the wall in the Day Hospital, encourage those waiting for treatment to "subscribe." We *do* have that choice even though it comes with great effort when so much potential adversity is present every day. Bill is feeling tired and weak today but receiving fluids which usually helps. Doctors ordered labs to monitor his levels and several key counts are very low. They sometimes offer transfusions for that, but he won't know until next Wednesday whether he will get that and/or round two of the new chemo. These lab results are unnerving and I'm feeling awfully vulnerable today—which is not helpful to Bill, so I'm calling on my Caring Bridge© peeps to pray for some "propping up" so I can be a stronger support to him.

> *We'll double up on today's prayers!*
>
> *—Cheryll*

> *Oh yes sending doubled triple doses for you to share. We have a ton of extra propping up thoughts and prayers to send your way as we know they will be put to good use.... get ready, here they come!*
>
> *—Louann*

> *Louann always puts thing so well. I'm with her. I can sort of say I know how you feel because my husband, Keith would be fairly good one day and pretty bad the next. Hang in there. Hopefully infusions and the good doctors will get him back on his feet.*
>
> *—Luana*

> *Thoughts and prayers for "propping" both you and Bill up. Thinking of you daily. Hugs!*
>
> *—Linda L*

> *Prayers and encouragement are what you need? Especially today? Needing propping up? We (the Caring Bridge Taters Crew) have got your back, your front, both sides, and top and bottom. Taters? I thought you'd never ask. We aren't Spec-Taters, or Commen-Taters or Agi-Taters. we are Participa -Taters. We will work overtime today.*
>
> *—Linda S*

I am with all your other Participa-Taters offering up prayers for "propping" you both up today...Prayer and Hugs..and some rousing Gospel music to lighten the load.

—Marcia L

Faith is the bird that feels the light and sings when the dawn is still dark. R. Jagore
From one of my favorite Susan Branch Illustrations/quotations.

—Nancy M

Marcia - I agree with the hymns. Listening to music is so soothing and uplifting. I'm praying for you both and thinking about you both. "Sometimes God calms the storm, and sometimes He lets the storm rage and calms His child." Am praying you can feel His peace, calmness and strength.

—Dawn

Crossing the "Ts" and Dotting the "Is"

June 8, 2018

We're reminded that being present in the moment is precious. Our world is so full of planning, being busy, and action oriented. That can really distract us from appreciating the "right now" in life. Last night we sat together and watched some TV (well, it was sports so I admit I did have a book) and at one point we commented on that simplicity and how nice it was to be together. How many couples miss that? If there is *any* beauty in our "now," it's the gratitude we have for realizing it.

Yesterday we talked with our Michigan oncologist about Bill's treatment and they agreed that they would follow the exact same protocol if he were home. The caveat for being here is the extra support they offer at the Cancer Center. We also received some links to potential clinical trials from Bill's sister and brother-in-law.

While Bill is not a likely candidate for a clinical trial because of his pulmonary embolisms, that literature also stated the course Bill is on matches what these links consider standard treatment. It's good to be thorough. We continue to make contact with other centers and hospitals. We pray this treatment will work to contain and destroy those cancer cells. So while we can be busy pursuing options, we can't lose sight of being present in the "now" of today.

> *Marcia, so well said. We all need to be more in the present and not dwell so much on what was or what's in the future. God Bless both of you.*
>
> *—Ginny*

> *So many times my prayers start with "Right now Jesus........... we need you."*
> *I am a big believer in the "right now".*
> *Love that you two are finding such comfort in each other. We will continue our "right now" prayers............ knowing*
> *He says "come to me all who are weary and I will give you rest." Love you both!*
>
> *—Sally R*

It is easy to stray from the moment. We educators are planners by nature with our lists and things to be done. So yes, focus on the good things no matter how small. Peace be with you!

—Debbie

I LOVE your comment on being present in the now of today! Well said! Love, hugs & blessings.

—Lisa D

Ups and Downs

June 10, 2018

Bill has wanted to see Aaron's apartment here in Milwaukee for three months and yesterday he felt well enough to head downtown. Zac was here, too, so the four of us drove into the "Third Ward," (a very cool neighborhood that has been through a beautiful gentrification) to see Aaron's apartment. Zac and I wandered down to the popular City Market to buy food for snacking and decided to have a drink and watch the Belmont Stakes. It was wonderful mom-son time! Meanwhile, Bill relaxed and watched golf (and the horse race) and he and Aaron had some one-on-one time, too. By the time we got back to Aaron's, Bill was ready to go home but really enjoyed himself. His eyes sparkled and he was peaceful. Today Bill is very tired and has more pain but the joy of yesterday lingers and makes both of us smile.

> *Wonderful to store up precious memories of close times together with our kids. You made us smile today and we send the smiles to you.*
>
> *—Linda S*

> *Great that both of you had special time with your sons. Although Bill is tired and has pain today, he can relive the joys of yesterday.*
>
> *—Ginny*

> *Prayers for more ups and less downs this week! I'm so glad you both had yesterday!*
>
> *—Sue*

It Feels Different Now

June 11, 2018

As we approached the Cancer Center today, we talked about how being here feels different now. Early on, we'd arrive thinking this is the path to healing. Now that the path has been diverted, it's hard to be as hopeful. It's an internal struggle every day to keep faith and trust God has a plan (I'd love to suggest a plan - but I know that's not for me to say.)

Today the focus is palliative care. While Bill got his fluids, the palliative care staff met with us to discuss pain management, side effects, fatigue, and diet. They upped pain management dosages so he's more comfortable and will continue to meet with us during chemotherapy. There is much to accomplish but we hope this will be helpful.

> *Sending hugs and prayers as you continue on this uncertain journey. May your faith stay strong. Enjoy all the little moments with a smile and a hug. Each day is a miracle!*
>
> *—Pam L*

> *Praying for you both. I was reading and came upon this and thought of you. "Storms will rock you –but won't sink you. God is not only for you – He is with you. Never let the presence of the storm cause you to doubt the presence of God."*
>
> *—Dawn*

> *Prayers for both of you and for the palliative care team as they help Bill be as comfortable as possible. They are experts at knowing what can help. Prayers also for hope. Maybe not the same kind of hope, but hope nonetheless. Hope for good days, good times, comfortable hours and time well spent for the two of you together and with loved ones, and hope that the current chemo is doing its job and destroying those cancer cells.*
>
> *—Sue*

Chasing After a Plan

June 14, 2018

When Bill couldn't have chemo Wednesday, I called his doctor to find out why. For the first time, we didn't get a call back. Today I called back and spoke to the nurse practitioner and learned: the doctor is gone for the week and they *did* call us back on our *Michigan landline* (despite the fact that our cells have been updated in their system as primary). This is so contrary to the excellent care we've had that I told the nurse how disappointed we are and that we feel no one cares about Bill's care now. It was probably a good release for me because I've been feeling pretty edgy. After that call, they offered labs, an appointment with the doctor, and chemo for Monday. I feel better. I believe I will serve enriched platelets for dinner every night until Monday just for good measure.

> *You go girl. You have to be an advocate for Bill. Not only does it help in his care but it helps you to know that you are able to do something and not just be a bystander. How are you serving the platelets? On the side or a main course?*
>
> *—Luana*

> *May I stop by for some of those yummy platelets? My supper suggestions sound pretty dull in comparison.*
>
> *—Marcia L*

> *At this point, some platelet cocktails might be just the thing. Good for you for being the "squeaky wheel!" In the medical world, people absolutely have to stand up for their loved ones!*
>
> *—Sue*

> *A girl's got to do what a girl's got to do. So glad you did this. They need to get it together; to be on the same page. You are an outstanding advocate.*
>
> *—Dawn*

> *That is such a coincidence because we had sautéed enriched platelets for lunch! Go figure.*
>
> *—Linda S*

> *You are fighting the good fight!! Way to take care of the situation! Sounds like you are serving determination with your platelets!! Nice job!!!*
>
> *—Lynne*

A Journal of Contrasts

June 18, 2018

Sunday was a lovely day for Bill. We went to Aaron's, Zac drove up (after just returning from a trip out west in the wee hours of the morning), and my sister Linda and her husband Steve joined us, too. We grilled salmon and all kinds of good food. It was a delightful day as we sat on the boardwalk of the river that flows out to Lake Michigan—with the US Open on a big screen TV. It was a very manly way to celebrate Father's Day!

Today Bill "qualified" for chemo since his platelets were at a normal level. The dose strength was reduced and the doctor cautioned that will be something to watch carefully— balancing side effects of blood thinners (medication for the clots) and giving enough muscle to the chemo so it will kill the bad cells. His bone marrow is pretty beaten up from all the treatments so we're hoping he can tolerate the chemo and his blood levels will maintain in the "OK" range. The yin and yang of life right now, all in one journal post.

> *Sounds like a lovely Father's Day. I can tell you are savoring these special moments. Wonderful. Praying for a great week. Let' s keep the positive momentum!*
> *—Diane*

> *Sounds perfect in many ways from the great Father's Day— to the news that he is ok to get the chemo. Nice to have some back to back good things come your way.*
> *—Louann*

> *Glad you could be on the water...so calming. Prayers and hugs to all.*
> *—Cindy H*

Family and Fluids

June 20, 2018

Bill's sister, Carolyn and brother-in-law, Jim arrived yesterday with Bill's mom who returned for a visit. They brought cherry pie from their home turf—Traverse City. It was delicious and Bill thoroughly enjoyed a slice. They're staying at a local hotel until Friday so we'll have lots of time to catch up. Bill has fluids today and that should "top off his tank" for a couple more hydrating days. The heavy rain has cleared out and milder temps are back. It's all good.

What a nice gathering for all and even the weather cooperated. Not to worry, we are getting the rain you sent packing. Thanks for the news

—Louann

You are an artist in so many ways. Your posts paint a picture of your circumstances whether good, scary, fun, silly, serious, or all of those plus more. It's almost as though we are at the window looking in and can see you two together or with family or company, hear your laughter and conversations, taste and smell those meals (especially that Traverse City cherry pie), and touch your belongings in your well decorated abode. You help us share it with you. We want to come in and laugh and cry with you, hug and fellowship together, and be in the presence of you both. Your posts are the next best thing. Thank you so much, friend.

—Linda S

So nice to have a wonderful family that has been so supportive. Enjoy your time with them plus the pie!! Take care and prayers to you both!!

—Cherryl

So glad you have family with you. Nothing better than cherry pie from Traverse City. Enjoy every moment.

—Dawn

Visitors are special but those who bring cherry pie from TC are awesome!

—Nancy H

What Took You So Long?

June 21, 2018

Last week Bill said, "I'm just giving this to God." We've done plenty of chasing, pursuing, and doors have closed. Not 24 hours passed and we got another lead with a certain amount of hope. We're not quite ready to share the details but suffice it to say: What took us so long? Complete trust and faith are our challenges as we walk the path as seekers of truth and God's plan. When we truly submit we prove our willingness to trust. The "reward" is our growing faith.

*And what an amazing journey you have had with mountaintops and valleys. You two are definitely an **inspiration** to many!*

—Marcia L

*Steven Furtick spoke about the fact that in a valley there are two mountains... and God lets us know that "there is the other side." I agree with you Marcia, that they are both such strong examples of praising Him in the valley, knowing that He is in charge of the journey! How awesome is it when we finally are able (and so crazy hard to do) to get out of His way. He is working in the waiting. He is orchestrating, teaching, maneuvering, growing us all through our waiting seasons. All He asks is that we stay faithful and praise Him "in" the storm. In **Jeremiah 12:3 (NIV)**"Yet you know me, O Lord. You see and test my thoughts about you.." In our season of struggle, waiting, and patience we know God is testing our hearts to see if we are staying true to Him. And then in **verse 5 (NIV)** God speaks back to Jeremiah saying, "If you have raced with men on foot, and they have worn you out, how can you compete with horses?" God is always working in our favor. He wants our faithfulness more than our happiness; yet with that faithfulness comes a happiness in Him that is far beyond anything else we could ever come up with! So....Bill and Marcia, take heart. You are being prepared to run with the horses! There is so much He has in store for you, so much we have no answers to, and yet with our faith and submission to Him, we see once again that He is crazy, madly in love with you....... So very awesome! Hang tough... stay strong...give it up to Him and then "saddle up!"*

—Sally R

Strong Will!

—Linda, Marcia's sister

The Lord always knows ways for our faith to be strengthened! "Let go and let God." Prayers continue. Take care and hugs!

—Cherryl

When we show God our faith - He shows us His faithfulness! Praying for a miracle!

—Dawn

Joining you in prayer that this is an open door.

—Lynne

As Good As It Is

June 22, 2018

Bill's mom, sister, and brother-in-law have been here visiting since Tuesday and left this morning to return home via Michigan's beautiful upper peninsula to Traverse City. They stayed at a nearby hotel and popped in for visits, meals, and conversation. Bill especially enjoyed seeing his sister Carolyn and brother-in-law Jim. They are very loving people and it's been a while since we've seen them. But anytime we (the "Queen's we," that is) entertain, we eat a bit too much, socialize a bit too much, and then it's time to pull back and chill. After fluids infusion today, Bill says he's headed home for some serious quiet time and some sleep. As good as it is to reconnect with those we love, it's important to "heed the need" for rest.

Now wasn't that poetic?

> *It is so nice to have family visit. A good nap is always nice also.*
>
> *—Debbie*

> *All good. Just another kind of good, and now time for all to digest how wonderful the visit and all connected with it was. Just savor it all.*
>
> *—Louann*

> *Company can be tiring even if you feel good as there is energy expended in being sociable. Happy it was a good time and at this point rest is important.*
>
> *—Ginny*

> *So nice that you both are able to enjoy the company of family and friends, important for everyone. Keep your faith, God is there with you both even when you need some extra rest, it's OK. God's blessings and continued prayers.*
>
> *—Pam L*

Another "Weak" End

June 24, 2018

Poor Bill! Saturday took us to the 24 Hour Cancer Center. Despite fluids on Friday, digestive issues wreaked havoc on him and we went in to get help. It's how he's reacting to this chemotherapy unfortunately. More fluids with added ingredients helped him feel better. An injection good for eight hours of relief lasted just that—eight hours. By last night he was miserable again. It's been a balancing act of eating things that are "safe" for the iffy belly and not irritating things. Today he's feeling a bit wiped out and very homebound, but it's a lovely day and the windows are wide open and a nice breeze is flowing through. Here's to a better tomorrow.

> *Praying for a better tomorrow and a solution to help Bill feel better more times than not. Marcia, I pray for you also, being upbeat as much as you are is not an easy task, I know. May God continue to wrap his arms around you as you continue to show us your loving grace in all you're dealing with yourself. Enjoy the breeze and sunshine.*
>
> *—Pam L*

> *Hoping tomorrow is better with the ups and downs of this disease and the treatments. Rely on your faith and know there are many pulling for you and Bill.*
>
> *—Ginny*

> *I'm so sorry about Bill's digestive troubles. It's got to be such a painful and uncomfortable feeling and being able to eat is so essential to our comfort and well-being. Prayers that this will get better and that Bill can find some things to eat that taste good and don't cause trouble.*
>
> *—Sue*

So Touching

June 26, 2018

Little Harrison is the four year old son of one of Aaron's friends. In fact, he and his daddy visited Bill a few weeks ago. Aaron went to see them last week end and while they were making dinner, Harrison asked if he could have the purple rubber band wrapping the asparagus. When asked why, he said "So I can have a purple bracelet like Daddy's." He'd noticed the 'Strong Will' band Justin wears for Bill and wanted to be just like him. There's just something special about a father/son bond.

> *And the good and love move on in ways we never imagined. How sweet and innocent.*
>
> *—Louann*

> *"Out of the mouths (and minds) of babes." If there's any good from this whole ordeal that you and Bill are going through, it's got to have something to do with the power of love.*
>
> *—Sue*

> *How sweet is that Marcia? Love the innocence of children. Have a peaceful day.*
>
> *—Julie J*

> *How wonderful! Kids are so sincere. Prayers continue.*
>
> *—Cherryl*

A Numbers Game

June 27, 2018

For Bill, much of his life has been about numbers: finance, funding, formulas...and many other complex categories that are more than I comprehend. Now, though, I'm eyeing the numbers: platelets, red cell count, white cell count, neutrophils. Simply put— there is a "good" range and a "not good" range. Carrying dread over numbers is a familiar feeling— I've <u>never</u> cared for numbers. But *these* numbers have a very different connotation. These numbers are a matter of life and death. The new "dread" is what will this lab work mean for chemo? While it's only Wednesday and chemo isn't scheduled until next Monday, Bill's platelets are lower today than they were Saturday. How they trend determines whether chemo is a go or not. There are five days between now and the next blood draw. Five days we can pray. Five days we can hope. Five days we can focus on those rising platelet numbers and try to find peace in breathing the same air.

> *Hoping for some nice high numbers in the days to come....frustrating to be doing all you can on the outside and yet the interior of his body is being stubborn. Hoping it gets back on track so moving ahead is possible come next week.*
>
> *—Louann*

> *Marcia and Bill, continue to pray for you daily (both of you). This is a very difficult journey but always remember that God is with you always. Please, please, please do not lose your hope. You are very strong individuals and prayers are coming from all over for both of you. God bless you and keep up the good fight. Love you both.*
>
> *—Dianna*

> *Prayers for solid numbers and strength for you both.*
>
> *—Valerie*

> *Five days to claim and proclaim a rise in those platelets!*
>
> *—Sally R*

> *Prayers for good numbers!! The people at my new church have been praying right along and I asked for more prayers before I read this because I knew from what you had written before that this is very difficult chemo.*
>
> *—Sue*

Five days we will pray and hope and focus with you, dear friends.

—Linda S

Waiting is awful, isn't it? Sometimes harder than the treatment. I hope you have some friends close by to vent to, to hug, and just be there - we here at home can only send virtual hugs but know they are all around you!

—Luana

While waiting, just enjoy each other. Thinking prayers while fondling my calculator. I'm pushing the + sign. Wish there was a way to drop off the minus sign. Love to both of you.

—Nancy M

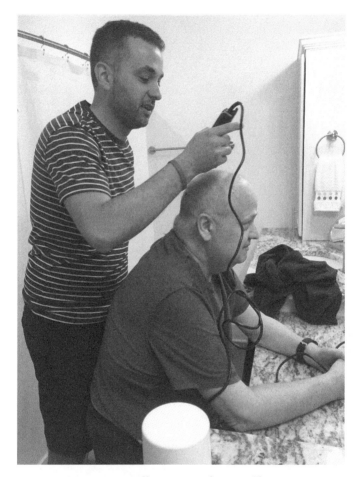

Aaron gives Bill an expert shave and haircut

Shave and a Haircut: Two Bits!

June 30, 2018

Anyone under the age of 40 probably has no clue about the meaning of this journal title, but it makes me smile.

Aaron stopped today and gave his dad a shave and a haircut. He said Bill always says "When you put on a suit, it makes you feel good!" Knowing Bill has felt pretty lousy for the past few days, he thought this was a *suit*able version of helping him to feel good. I think it worked!

> *How nice of Aaron! Maybe he has found a new profession! Bill, you look good! Take care and prayers continue.*
>
> *—Cherryl*

> *Looking pretty handsome Bill . So lucky to have a talented young man in the family. Take care. Blessings to you both.*
>
> *—Julie J*

> *Bill, you look great! Praying for you and your family.*
>
> *—Dawn*

> *Bill looks great! There must be no end to Aaron's talent. He looked like an awesome chef a while ago and now a barber to boot.*
>
> *—Sue*

Visits Matter

July 1, 2018

There have been 8,840 visits to Bill's Caring Bridge© site since it started in November. Thanks to my sister Linda who knew about this online tool for informing friends and loved ones about an illness or concern for someone, we have been able to keep others up to date on Bill. Wow! What awesome support from all you "Bridge Supporters."

I'm wondering how long it will take to reach 10,000?

[Note: At the book publication time there were over 15,000 visits to the website.]

> *Messages give you and Bill something to look forward to just as we look forward to your messages. Appreciate keeping us updated.*
>
> —*Ginny*

> *I think you need a recount. Every time I visit the site I read it to Jim and we often discuss the comments. Shouldn't that count for double?*
>
> —*Linda S*

> *Amazing but not surprising as you keep so many of us in the loop at a time. I have done this with a few family and friends with nowhere near that many followers. We will be over that number in no time as we all love challenges, don't we? You two are having the biggest one but still we are all in!*
>
> —*Louann*

> *8841!*
>
> —*Sally R*

Freedom

July 4, 2018.

Bill's pain was unmanageable at home so he spent Monday and Tuesday in the hospital and finally it's under control. Now we're playing with a balance of mental clarity and keeping his pain minimized. We're getting the hang of it slowly. Bill's fragile system cannot tolerate a full dose of chemo and this lighter dose is not working— so that will probably be discontinued. We'll meet with the oncologist tomorrow along with palliative care to see what other tricks might be up their sleeves.

On this day when freedom is celebrated in our country, we realize we have the personal freedom to choose how we respond to this news. Despite the many doors that have slammed in our faces, we are grateful for each other. I savor the sweetness of lying next to Bill in bed listening to his soft breathing and the warmth of his body near mine. These are the struggles we face— mighty though they are. Being present in today— right now— is what we must do.

> *I'm so sorry that Bill's pain has gotten so bad and about the bad news on the chemo. Prayers for good ideas from the oncologist and for a peaceful and restful night for both of you.*
>
> *—Sue*

> *Sorry the chemo treatments aren't doing what was hoped for. The moments you share together on this journey show all of us your unending love. May there be some answers for you tomorrow as you look forward to the time ahead. Praying for God's peace and comfort for both of you.*
>
> *—Pam*

> *Heartbreaking...bittersweet...unending hope...*
>
> *—Lynne*

> *Oh dear, another challenge when you have faced so many ups and downs on this journey. So good, that even with this news, you are able to see and appreciate the small things you have control over, like the quiet time of just been physically close. Continue to savor those times with each other.*
>
> *—Louann*

Our hearts are heavy for you both. Although we have never had to face a time as challenging as yours, we have always had each other to cling to throughout our darkest days. We are so happy that you have that love and closeness with Bill. There is strength and comfort in that. It is a special gift from God.

—Linda S

Insomnia

July 7, 2018

I can't sleep. Another night of "monkey brain." I worry. I fret. I try praying. It's a funny thing how night brings the wolves to the door. Bill has so much pain and we're trying to get on a good schedule to manage that. Now he has a persistent cough that started with his hospital stay this week. I'll call the Cancer Center when it's fully light and maybe they will have something to help. All these symptoms breed fear. Shame on me for not being able to let it go, lay it in God's lap, and find peace. The sun is starting to rise and the birds are beginning to chirp. Today looms large and scary and I'm praying for the strength to embrace it.

With the light of day find peace in Him.... He promises that He is enough! So easy to say...so hard to trust... thus comes faith in the wait. Fervent and bold prayers for you already sent this morning. Accept and claim them! Hugs.
—Sally R

Of course you have "monkey brain." Your heart and mind are full. Wish I could be there to give you a hug. May you find peace today and may Bill be pain free. I'm so sorry that prayers are all I have to offer, but know you are both in them.

—Diane

There is no shame in being the human that you are. In fact, you have been above and beyond human throughout this time. Please give yourself a break and try and feel the love and concern that is coming your way in this battle that seems to be all uphill for you at this point. If only any of us could take some of this from you it would happen in a second. But, your feelings, as well as Bill's, come from the love you share. Stay strong as you are able to feel your way through this. We all wish we could do something as we know you would for us.
—Louann

No shame needed friend. This Bible verse has offered comfort at times when I didn't know how or what or when to pray or just simply couldn't pray. **Romans 8:26** *(NIV) says: "In the same way the Spirit helps us in our weakness. We don't know what we ought to pray for, but the Spirit himself intercedes for us with groans that words cannot express." I am asking the Holy Spirit to pray your prayers for you as long as needed. He will find your words and speak them for you. Have peace, dear ones.*

—Linda S

Sometimes Caregivers Need a Time Out

July 7, 2018

I guess you can't run on empty. I felt awful today. I was exhausted, ached all over, and had zero energy— probably from my messed up sleep pattern. Zac came to visit this afternoon and it was *the* best help for us both. I was horizontal much of the day while Zac helped with meals, kept Bill company and assisted him, too, so I could sleep. What perfect timing! It was such a huge help to be able to catch my breath and rest. Tonight it's quiet and we're just enjoying the peace.

> *I'm so glad you were able rest! It's hard to take care of yourself when you are giving your all for another! Heaven sent you an angel today.*
>
> *—Claudia.*

> *So happy you were able to get some rest. Caregivers need to also take care of themselves so they are able to function. Glad Zac was there to give a helping hand. Next time he is there tell him I said hi and take care of his mom.*
>
> *—Ginny*

> *Sending prayers to you Marcia— so glad Zac could come to visit and give you some time to rest. Peace.*
>
> *—Cindy M*

> *God sent an angel (Zac) to help you both. Prayers continue for you and your family!! Take care.*
>
> *—Cherryl*

"Chefs" Aaron and Zac prepare dinner for us

A Mixed Day

July 9, 2018

Poor Bill has pneumonia! He had a cough that started right after he left the hospital last Tuesday and it was confirmed at the hospital this morning. He's home with antibiotics and resting tonight. The "boys" (Aaron and Zac) were amazing. They bought groceries and Zac again whipped up some dinner while I did nothing to help. I'm lots better today so whatever it was yesterday must have been a "hit and run." Grateful we are where we are tonight.

Oh boy, lots of fluids and keep taking those meds. Those two guys are amazing. So glad they are with you. Just rest up. Praying for you all.

—Dawn

*As the realities of daily life happen all around you— fatigue, sickness, flu, awesomeness of your sons, the joy of "being" with Bill....always remember that you are constantly learning and teaching...both are critical to your journey. The **most** important is that you are finding time to be still and know that He is God...and He has already overcome all of this. So learn on, teach on, and listen on! Love, prayers and hugs!*

—Sally R

So sorry to learn of pneumonia, but happy the boys were there to help and that you are feeling better. Prayers.

—Ginny

Stay strong and carry on. Use your support guys as much as you can. They love you so much! My prayers are ever with you.

—Kris

What a blessing to have your boys nearby. I pray for you daily and still hope that God's will is your will. If it isn't, I pray that He is with you always, giving you what you need.

—Elizabeth (Liz)

Improving

July 10, 2018

I feel elated when Bill feels better. Yesterday he said his cough was better, he *felt* better, and at one point he was pain free. As the day progressed his color improved and his interactions were perkier. Good old antibiotics are doing their job. So grateful for these moments because so many others are tough and really tax the stamina.

> *One praise report at a time. That is all He asks!*
>
> —*Sally R*

> *The sun is shining, the birds are chirping, your prayer team is rallying, Bill is feeling better, you have some bits of relief. Grateful.*
>
> —*Cindy H*

> *Wow. Quick change in the right direction is no small thing. Cherish the time and know we are grateful for the meds kicking the pain demons as well as getting the infection reigned in. Indeed a good hump day to bask in this positive report.*
>
> —*Louann*

> *Wonderful news!! Prayers for continued healing.*
>
> —*Cherryl*

> *It is just that simple and yet that profound.*
>
> —*Lynne*

> *Thank the Lord for meds. So glad he had a good day!!!*
>
> —*Dawn*

Go West Young Man

July 11, 2018

We are going to Scottsdale, Arizona to see if there is further treatment for Bill. There is a clinic where there has been some progress treating pancreatic cancer and there may be a clinical trial for Bill. It's a long shot—we know, but we're asking for prayers to guide us through this last frontier. We leave Sunday morning and return Thursday. If there is nothing they can offer, we will have seen a beautiful part of the country and shared more precious time together.

And then we will go home.

Nothing to be lost and so much may be gained: possible treatment and, like you say, seeing a wonderful part of the country. You two have the best attitude in spite of many dark days. Wishing and praying for some restful moments and another avenue you have explored...

—Louann

Prayers are a given. I hope you can find the answers you are looking for.

—Luana

I send prayers and love and hope as you travel west. I hope you can feel all of us cheering you forward in your journey!

—Gretchen

Prayers for a safe and productive trip. You and Bill have both been so open at looking at all of the possibilities. The dry, warm air in Arizona may be helpful for the pneumonia also.

—Sue

Safe travels and I pray for good news. Someone needs to conquer this awful cancer!

—Barbara

Praying for God's healing hand to be laid upon you in Scottsdale. It is a beautiful area, enjoy your precious time away as you look at a possible different way to beat this cancer, Prayers and hugs.

—Pam L

Jesus...right now! We need your amazing grace and your powerful promises. We praise you in the middle of this storm, and call your name for safe travel and a perfect fit for this new study... claiming it all in Your Name!

—Sally R

Forever praying for just one miracle—and safe travels.

—Linda, Marcia's sister

Just love your enduring spirit and faith! Joining you all in prayer for healing and safe travels in Jesus' name.

—Lynne

Are We Sorry?

July 12, 2018

Our pastor from Michigan called to catch up with us and during the conversation asked if we were sorry we'd made the move to Milwaukee with the latest outcome. It's a sensible query: we were "all in," took the chance, gave the "wheel a spin," and "busted." (That's an awful lot of Las Vegas talk, isn't it?)

No. We're not sorry. Granted we didn't get the desired outcome but we *did* satisfy any lingering doubt— wondering if we hadn't come here what *might* have happened. And the richness of being truly together forging through this has been very precious. Tough, yes. Exhausting, yes. But it's brought us so much closer (if that's possible) and I'll always be grateful for that. Along the way we've met many great people who are passionate about their work to help people with cancer and treat and cure them.

No. We're not sorry.

> *Interesting question for sure. You'll always have the satisfaction of knowing that you've left no stone unturned. You both have fought this dreadful disease with everything you have.*
>
> *—Sue*

> *You have chosen wisely: from good information, intelligence and love. Not sorry, indeed.*
>
> *—Linda S*

> *What wonderful Faith you both have. Thinking of you both. LOVE, hugs and peace be with you.*
>
> *—Cindy M*

> *You had to go. ..give it your all...and you realized it is all about the journey TOGETHER. What a blessing you have in each other. Not to sound flip— but tally ho! Scottsdale it is. Hope there is good news there. Prayers continue. Love and hugs.*
>
> *—Cindy H*

A Faith Visit

July 14, 2018

Tonight, out of the blue, a lovely woman who lives here in Wisconsin called me. She's a P.E.O., an organization I also belong to, and heard about us from someone in the chapter I've attended while we are here. Her husband was recently diagnosed with pancreatic cancer and we had a wonderful talk. How fortuitous! The stories are so similar: a wonderful marriage, a shocking diagnosis, a shared faith in God: instant friendship. In spite of the immense challenges, along the way we have these beautiful opportunities to connect with others. It's a "sign" I'm sure— that we are not alone in this journey. Tomorrow we leave for Arizona. We're asking for prayers for safe travel and miraculous possibilities. We know our Caring Bridge© followers have our backs. Keep those prayers flowing.

> *Know that you are surrounded by prayers for safe travel and for miraculous possibilities.*
>
> *—Marcia L*

> *We got your backs, fronts, both sides, tops and bottoms. Go with God, dear ones.*
>
> *—Linda S*

> *Remember the saying you were a part of "Endless Possibilities?" I'm praying for those for you this week. Safe and comfortable travels. Thanks for taking the time each day to keep this journal and share your faith journey. Love and hugs to you both.*
>
> *—Cindy H*

> *Safe travels. God speed and Jesus take the wheel! God's got this!*
>
> *—Sally*

> *Praying for safe travels and for healing.*
>
> *—Dawn*

> *May you both encounter even more "angels" on this journey. Thinking and praying for both of you.*
>
> *—Debbie*

Arizona Arrival

July 16, 2018

Yesterday's flight from Milwaukee was uneventful and yet we found ourselves really exhausted when we got to the hotel. The surroundings are beautiful with many plants, cacti, and desert flowers dotting the landscape. Our accommodations are serene and give Bill a pleasant place to rest. Today we're checked in at the doctor's waiting for Bill's consult. As the day unfolds, I'll share the news we have.

Oh Marcia – praying for you and Bill.

—Dawn

*I'm sure you are beyond exhausted, physically, mentally, emotionally with all that has been happening. Maybe the peacefulness others find in the landscape will be a nice antidote. While **our** growing things are dying from the heat, Arizona has such resilient colors- the cacti and some of the trees that I remember. Thoughts, hopes and magic wishes are all right there from Michigan to Arizona.*

—Louann

It's so different from what we're used to seeing. Prayers that this consultation goes well and that you and Bill can get some good rest.

—Sue

What's Next?

July 16, 2018

There are two viable options for clinical trials. Tomorrow doctors will biopsy spots on his liver to gather cancer cells which will help determine which trial is best for him. It will likely mean another relocation and we have many questions before we move forward. As we make decisions we will share the game plan. In the meantime, please continue to pray for God to reveal a course for us and that healing is part of this plan.

> *Happy that you and Bill have other options. Positive thoughts coming to you.*
>
> —*Nancy H*

> *Prayers for wisdom for the doctors and for you and Bill! Also prayers that the biopsy goes well today.*
>
> —*Sue*

> *We are praying that the Great Physician will guide your thinking and your decisions and lead you to a path towards healing.*
>
> —*Linda S*

Another "Weighting" Room

July 17, 2018

Bill is having his liver biopsy. The familiarity of this is too much. He is so courageous and it seems one of these "procedures" should yield something positive. All I can do is wait. The waiting rooms are all the same-whether in Michigan, Wisconsin, or Arizona. It's a lonely vigil. I worry as do others in this space. But most of all, I pray for God to guide the doctors in their care for Bill, his protection, and healing. These prayers are old friends. Amid all of this, I hope for answers. In the heat of this beautiful desert day where it will soar to 105 degrees, I look at the world God has created and think, "Surely a God who has created such an awesome world has a little good news for Bill."

> *Praying for both you and Bill right now! Asking God for good news and peace as you wait.*
>
> *—Linda L*

> *You always have positive thoughts so we stand behind you 100%. Positive thoughts bring positive results! Are one of the boys there with you? Keep us posted as I know you will. We prayer warriors are giving out the battle cry here in Michigan. Go Bill! Go Marcia! Go medical staff! Get this healing started!*
>
> *—Luana*

> *Storming the heavens. May the God of all being envelop you.*
>
> *—Pat S*

> *We are always with you in thoughts and prayer!*
>
> *—Claudia*

> *I have been thinking of you both all day. Praying!*
>
> *—Cherryl*

> *May God hold you in the palm of His hand.*
>
> *—Ginny*

> *Praying for healing and good news for both of you! Hope Arizona has the answers you want and need!!*
>
> *—Barbara*

Reflective Truth

July 18, 2018

It's early morning in Arizona. I'm sitting outside on the patio while it's still cool enough to enjoy it. Bill is catching a few more winks before an appointment with the doctor to discuss some logistics and details of potential next steps.

A woman named Christine Caine was diagnosed with cancer. She said to her doctor, "Well, one of three things will happen: God will cure me, medical treatment will cure me, or I will die and God will take me home (and I'll be cured). Either way, it's a win."

Her words struck me because of their simple truth. It's replacing fear with faith. What continues to be powerful in this journey is to share the testimony of followers who band together to be witnesses in faith. I know this helps me and I'm sure it does others. Caring Bridge© is a tool to share, organize, and record. But it's so much more when the responses from those who subscribe leave the rich feedback for us to experience and savor.

> *You have very wise words for us today. Prayers that Bill has a positive consultation with the doctor. You and Bill are walking down a road that none of us ever want to be on, but many of us will at some point in our lives. The two of you are showing us how to do it with faith, grace and dignity. Peace to both of you!*
>
> —*Sue*

> *Thank you for being Marcia, the teacher, today. Thank you for sharing what you have learned and are learning from this unique experience. We are your students as well as your prayer warriors and support team.*
>
> —*Linda S*

> *Thank you for sharing your faith journey, it truly is a blessing to keep up with you & Bill through this website. It is wonderful to witness the hand of God and all the prayers and support for you and your family.*
>
> —*Cindy M*

> *You are spot on with your message today. The Lord knows where our paths lead us and he will comfort us along the way. Prayers continue!! Take care.*
>
> —*Cherryl*

Thank you for sharing your lessons on this journey that we will all take. As Linda said, you were our wise teacher today. Praying for you both.

—Diane

Through Caring Bridge we are all part of your journey. The thoughts / prayers your friends share are testimony to you and Bill and to everyone who journeys with you. Bountiful Blessings today as you go forward together.

—Marcia L

The Next Chapter

July 20, 2018

We arrived back in Milwaukee in the wee hours of the morning. The clinical trials in Arizona will not work for Bill, so we press on. We're planning to move home next Monday. Our boys will come on the weekend and do the heavy lifting— bless them. We will load what we can into our car and go. It will be interesting to see what home is like after all this time, the yard work, and all the silly little things that are just every day routine when you're there. We've heard the road in our subdivision has been resurfaced so that will be nice to enjoy. Apartment living is certainly less complicated.

We have appointments lined up in Michigan for next week and some leads we've yet to pursue. It's with a mixture of feelings we will leave. Bill has had such outstanding care here and everything is so close. Commuting from home will be an adjustment again. Being close to home, family, and friends will be a welcome blessing as there is a certain lonesomeness to living here. It puts so much pressure on the loved ones who *are* close. But even though the doors are closing, I still see a very small crack of light underneath. Call me a moth, but I'm drawn to it and going after what is to be found.

> *Prayers continue for you and Bill every day. Also, prayers for a safe journey home. You must be exhausted! I'm sure it will be good to be back HOME again.*
>
> *—Linda L*

> *Traveling mercies as you travel back home with heavy hearts and excitement to be back in your home again. May you have many angels back home that can help you settle in. Gods blessings as you continue to pursue what's in that little crack of light under the door. Praying for comfort and peace for you both.*
>
> *—Pam L*

> *Safe travels, it will feel good to be home. The normalness will help you process and relax.*
>
> *—Valerie*

I'm sorry things didn't work out in Arizona as you had hoped. Thank goodness for your boys stepping up to the plate. Their kindness and willingness to help shows what great young men you've raised. Many people here are anxious to have you home and want to help with whatever you and Bill need. Prayers for some good rest for both of you. Try not to worry about all of the things that have to be done in moving back. It will all work itself out.

—Sue

We have such mixed feelings. Sad that you didn't get the answers you were seeking, but relieved that you will soon be back in familiar surroundings. What will not change when you get home are the love, prayers and support we send daily.

—Linda S

Home: Leaving and Returning

July 22, 2018

A sweet summer breeze wafts through the windows tonight as we gather our things in Wisconsin and anticipate going home tomorrow. When we moved in on March 1st, a snowstorm blasted us that first night!

The boys were here over the week end and so was my sister Linda. They helped pack and load what we will take in the car. On Friday the boys will return and load a small truck with what's left to take to Michigan.

In spite of the immense disappointments we've faced, our little spot here has been a beautiful respite and place to rest. Our relationship is stronger than ever and for that I'm grateful. We've met wonderful people and some to whom we will be forever connected. We carry those good memories and experiences with us as we go forward. Bill has heard from friends who are eager to see him once he is home so his "calendar" is filling for later in the week. As evening settled in, Bill remarked, "I feel the best I've felt in a week!"

It sounds like the decision to go home is a good one.

> As you sat to write that post...where to start must have come to your mind a few times. Such a journey you never expected. Lessons you were taught, and as the forever teacher that you are...you taught us all such incredible lessons about loving each other, loving life, and loving God. Your journey together has been a powerful statement of who you are and how you have chosen to live faithfully praising him directly in the middle of this storm. We all stand with you now as you make your way to Michigan to reconnect with many. Safe travels and may God's hedge of protection blanket your trip. We will continue the fervent prayers and the claims of His promises of hope and a future as well as the amazing prayer of knowing He has given us a heart to know Him and rest in His peace and grace..... and that carries us more confidently through the next chapter of your love story. Until we talk in Michigan... love, hugs and God speed, you two!
>
> —Sally R

Welcome home after your search brings you back to us. With your return you are bringing such experiences and connections and the ability to see and be seen by many of us. Sounds like you will need nap time to keep your energy, given the lineup that wants to see you. Safe travels.

—Louann

A still smiling tuckered Bill, heading back to Michigan

Feeling the Love

July 23, 2018

We're home! The drive was easy and we ran into Sally and Don, two friends from home at a service plaza on the toll road. Once we got home, our *ultra*-super neighbors, Bob and Cindy hustled over to help unload the car, brought some lovely snacks and treats, and had a gorgeous outdoor plant on our front step to welcome us. We are so blessed! They are terrific people and right next door. My daughter Jenn came over with some groceries, helped me put things away, and made it so much easier to tackle the piles. She's just what I needed—plus it was great to see her after this long time away. Bill went to bed almost immediately because he was awfully tired after the long ride today. Tomorrow he can just rest and I will be the busy bee getting more things settled until the final load on Saturday.

One of my favorite spots at home is the screened porch overlooking the backyard and pond. Aaron's good friend, Brandon, wanted to do something to help so he borrowed a key, took down the storm windows, and arranged the furniture on the porch and deck so we could enjoy it right away. What a sweet thing to do! It's been just a matter of hours and we're so touched by the love and kindness we've experienced. Time for bed but after prayers of thanks!

> *It seems like you are getting back what you two put out. People happy to be helpful in ways you can truly use right now. The state of Michigan is very happy to have you back in our country and out of the dairy state!*
>
> —*Louann*

> *Welcome Home! May you be continually showered with many blessings. I'm so glad your lovely porch was ready for you. Enjoy :-)*
>
> —*Pat*

> *How wonderful to have such loving and thoughtful friends. It makes me happy to hear how much you and Bill are cared for. Home is best.*
>
> —*Diane*

> *What a wonderful Homecoming you've had! Home is still the best place to rest and rejuvenate. Enjoy your view from the deck....How fun to see Sally and Don ...your first hometown greeters!*
>
> —*Marcia L*

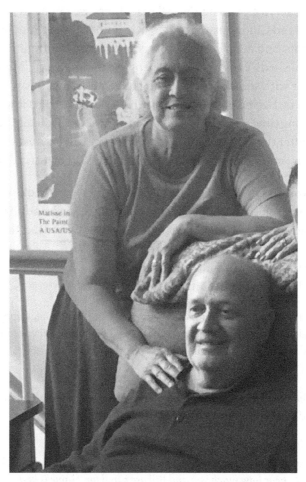

Bill with his sister Carolyn as she helps us settle back in at home

Resetting the Direction

At Bill's consult with his oncologist, he learned the doctor wants to get him set up at Karmanos in Detroit to see what clinical trials are available for Bill. We're a couple weeks out from that appointment and that's nerve wracking because we know time is of the essence. Meanwhile, he is scheduled for fluid hydration at home and Bill's sister and brother-in-law are here for a couple of days. Fatigue has descended on him *big time*. He is so weary. Rest is the treatment of the hour and we're hoping it will rejuvenate him so he's able to enjoy being home. Keep praying for us! We press on.

> *Prayers continue, enjoy visits with family and friends, they can lift your spirits. May you find comfort and peace while you continue to look for options.*
> —Pam L

> *Prayers for rest for Bill and for you as well. Karmanos has offered hope and the gift of time to many. Prayers that they will have some good options for Bill.*
> —Sue

Men With A Truck

July 27, 2018

The plan for the final move back home was that Zac and Aaron would pack what didn't fit in the car into a truck and drive here by tomorrow night. Well, those two overachievers had everything packed shortly after noon CST today and are a couple of hours away. An amazing feat! Zac managed to sell all the furniture we bought and planned to get rid of in Wisconsin— but still the truck was very full. It's amazing what accumulated in just under six months. Bless those boys! We are *so* grateful for the help. A new friend returned the cable TV equipment which saved the boys an extra trip and helped us tremendously (Thank you, Liz!)

Bill received fluids at the local hospital warmly welcomed by the nurses who took care of him before our move. He is so weak and tired and uncomfortable but wants to be awake when the guys arrive tonight. Carolyn and Jim (Bill's sister and brother-in-law) helped with *many* things around the house today and delivered a new set of wheels for Bill to borrow – a very spiffy walker. It gives him lots of stability and the timing is perfect. We focus on gratitude for all these bounteous gifts tonight— love, support, and the caring of loved ones.

> *I live near you now. I would be glad to help out in any way that you need. I can run errands for you or keep Bill company so that you can get out. Just know that I'm available and you both have been and will continue to be in my prayers. Don't hesitate to reach out.*
>
> *—Debbie L*

> *It's wonderful that you have some great support! It's very true when they say, "No one fights alone." The help you receive is not only a blessing to you and Bill. It's a blessing to those who do the "helping."*
>
> *—Sue*

> *I'm happy to know that you are comfortably settled at home, with friends and family nearby to support you.*
>
> *—Diane*

Both of you have obviously given so much to so many, for so long. As much as you think it does not feel "right" you are reaping what you have sown. And you know, by doing that, with the grace and thankfulness you both exhibit, continue to give the opportunity to so many. Be well and take care, both of you.

—Louann

Love those boys! They continue to be such good help for both of you.

—Debbie

So happy to hear you are home. Family is wonderful!!

—Cherryl

Integrating the Accumulation

July 29, 2018

You may think you're living efficiently, but when it comes off a truck and back into your house you feel really grateful for the extra hands to help put it all away. Zac, the birthday boy, Aaron, Aaron's friend Brandon, Carolyn and Jim all pitched in to help settle us back in. Bill slept a lot yesterday, the aftermath of recent meds. By last night he was able to join the conversation and relax with us as we enjoyed peanut butter pie, in lieu of a birthday cake for Zac. It was a very productive day and this morning everyone is sleeping a little later except me, the resident insomniac. Even Melatonin seems to be resisting me. Maybe it's the other way around.

I'm resisting Melatonin!

> *Sometimes our heart over rules the benefits of some sleep aid. We are so happy and grateful to be in our own space with those who mean so much to us under the same roof. We do not want to waste a minute being in bed when we can be up and just enjoying the quiet and familiar surroundings in a place that just oozes love...enjoy and you will be able to grab a nap when both your body and head say time to pause and hit the reset button.*
>
> *—Louann*

> *What would we do without family and friends? At least you are in one place now. We hope that much needed rest will come soon.*
>
> *—Ginny*

> *May God give you the strength you need to fight! And may he bless your family with comfort in knowing He has an ultimate plan. We are always thinking of you all. And we wish and pray for you all! Love you all!*
>
> *—Todd*

Sepsis

July 30, 2018

Bill has sepsis. We are in the local emergency room waiting to be admitted. We will be transferred to Beaumont Hospital from here as soon as all tests come back. It was a productive day: the boys tackled several projects while Jenn helped hang blinds on the porch. We're lucky to have such great kids! Brother-in-law Jim and Bill's sister Carolyn got meals and handled clean up. But amid all that, Bill was very tired and *just wanted to sleep*. He was also disoriented but we thought it was the aftermath of medication he was given Friday. Now we know! We're waiting for more test results and Jenn is poised and ready to drive me to or from the hospital. A familiar setting in the wee hours of the morning. Prayers are appreciated, Caring Bridge© followers.

Sending prayers!

—*Carrie*

Hang in there! Prayers for a speedy recovery from sepsis. So glad your children are so attentive and helpful. Prayers and more prayers. ...

—*Cindy H*

I'm so sorry about this! Prayers that they will get this under control for Bill. We said prayers for you and Bill today at church.

—*Sue*

Praying for strength for all of you.

—*Debbie*

So sorry to hear. Know what you are going through. John had sepsis last August and again in December. It is amazing what drugs will do. Thank goodness for our kids. Stay strong and continued prayers.

—*Ginny*

Grateful for your family. Such strong support ..and sending prayers for quick control of sepsis.

—*Marcia L*

So glad you're surrounded with love and support.. Prayers will continue.

—*Pam P*

Sadness Descends

July 30, 2018

Tonight Bill is at Beaumont. He's had lots of medical professionals observing, caring for, and treating him. Jenn drove here in case I needed a ride home since I rode with Bill in the ambulance. The most serious concern is that Bill's liver is failing. It is very, very grave. Bill's brother, Sam and wife Cathy came today and are staying. His brother Tom is coming tomorrow as are Jim, Carolyn and Bill's mom, Rita. Aaron is on his way and will come tomorrow. Niece Mackenzie stopped after work which brought a smile to Bill's face. Lastly, we had a visit from Barb and Gary, good friends. The comfort of many is great. Please pray, friends.

> *Thoughts and prayers & strength through all that you have endured... please know we are here. You have many around you ... so we will keep our distance hoping though you feel the peaceful energy we are sending.*
> *—Shannon*

> *Not the news any of us want to hear or read. But knowing the two of you have had some incredible moments together on this roller coaster of health, emotions, moves, etc. Now you are able to spend some quiet time in the space your love has created. May this be a time you can find courage and peace.*
> *—Louann*

> *Saddened by the news, may all of you find comfort from angels near and far. Prayer for the comfort in God's love for you both and your family. You both have gone the extra mile on this journey. Be still and know that God will be with you always. Hugs and love, my friends.*
> *—Pam L*

> *Jim and I and so many others will pray you through whatever is ahead, whether great rejoicing or great sadness or both.*
> *—Linda S*

> *May God's grace and comfort continue to sustain you. Rest assured He has you in His arms.*
> *—Don*

Great Uncertainties

July 31, 2018

Early morning hours brought Aaron- all the way from Milwaukee where he is still working - to see Bill. It's always a great joy for him. In his fuzziness Bill asked, "What are you doing here?" We smiled at each other because we know when those we love are in need, where else would we be? He will be moved from ICU to the regular floor of the hospital today. Jenn texted early with her gracious offer to gather any things we need from the house and will be the courier to Beaumont.

As dawn broke vitals were stable but the concern is for Bill's blood to clot appropriately so they can aspirate and he can get some relief from the fluid buildup in his belly. Still the liver continues to be under attack with disease progression.

Today will be a day of visitors for a man who loves so richly. May it be soothing for him to have a little glimpse of how loved he is.

> *Good to see his humor has not ebbed under the recent events. And you? Stronger than I am sure you ever imagined. But we all knew that about you individually and united it is a formidable force of two and added to that are all of us on the cheering/praying band wagon. Of course, like others, just a phone call away for anything that needs doing, xx*
> > —*Louann*

> *Sending my love and prayers to all!!! Big hugs too!*
> > —*Sharon*

> *Prayers for some relief from the fluid buildup and maybe some rest for you. I hope the visitors bring Bill some comfort.*
> > —*Sue*

> *Praying Bill is alert enough to enjoy all his company. It's always nice to know how much one is loved. God's Blessings!*
> > —*Pam L*

> *So glad to hear family is with you. The Lord will be your strength, and comfort you through this. Praying.*
> > —*Cherryl*

The Gang's All Here

August 1, 2018

Family descended yesterday: siblings Carolyn and Jim, Sam and Cathy, Tom, Linda and Amy. Bill's mom who is nearly 93 years old is confused about all that is happening. Our kids, Aaron, Jenn and Zac are here to support in any way they can while nieces Chelsea and Mackenzie round out the roster. Such love!

Bill was moved from ICU last night to a semi private room but it was miserable. It was a tight space with a roommate who constantly coughs and watches TV late into the night. I stayed with Bill and it was a dreadful night for both of us. This morning he is getting an ultra-sound of the abdomen and we're hoping they can relieve the fluid buildup in the belly. Liver function numbers worsen and we're praying for some good news today.

Right now I'd be grateful for a toothbrush.

> *Jeepers, this is not a time to ask "what next or what else can happen?" Especially after such wonderful care and surroundings in Wisconsin and then a bit of home sweet home this must seem particularly harsh. Might be time to call in the social worker or the hospice coordinator at the hospital. Maybe nothing can be done, but that seems unlikely and would be good if it could happen. You both need rest and a soothing spot for all to come to. A benefit for the roommate who has a whole different kind of body rhythm going on. A toothbrush can be had from the nurse/aide etc. or at the least the gift shop. It really does get down to the little things that can make life so much nicer which is a true benefit at this moment. In my thoughts, all of you!*
> *—Louann*

> *What an ordeal. Louann always mirrors my thoughts but she can express them so much better than I can. Since so much family is there maybe you can sneak away for a bit - sit in a quiet place - and calm you spirit. People tend to think that the only answer to your prayer from God is yes and if it isn't a yes they say God doesn't listen, God didn't hear my prayer. Yes, he always hears our prayers but like a parent - sometimes the answer is no. He has a plan for Bill and for you. I know how awful it is to see your spouse suffer but through all of it you have to remember God loves you both.*
> *—Luana*

So happy that you are surrounded by love and family! I hope they can drain that fluid and make Bill a whole lot more comfortable. I hope you get your toothbrush, toothpaste and all of the necessities that you need. Sometimes it's the little things....

—Sue

Everyone's words are so thoughtful and meaningful. You are both so loved and we are all praying that God will provide peace and everything you need to continue this journey. I pray that you can feel His loving arms around you holding you when you feel you cannot endure anymore. Much love to you both.

—Elizabeth (Liz)

May God be ever so near to give Bill comfort and for the whole Wright family peace during this very tough time.

—Pam L

Finding Peace

August 1, 2018

A day of complexities: Bill had a procedure called a celiac nerve block. It deadens the nerve receptors so he feels less pain which often accompanies pancreatic cancer. He sleeps tonight sedated. Gloriously, niece Cassie arrived and saved the day quite literally. She was able to get Bill back into a private room with her silver tongue of persuasion. It is serene and quiet and we're grateful. Tomorrow morning they will finally aspirate fluid from his abdominal area and that should also offer more relief for his discomfort. After that, we will see what the doctors say.

He is quiet these days. Conversation is minimal and I sense he is pondering what lies ahead. There is a detachment and a distance as he prepares. The sadness is overwhelming. Anticipating what may be much sooner than any of us hoped is devastating. Yet I would be selfish to try and interfere. I love this man so much and deeply admire his effort to keep going despite the bad news and negative results he has experienced over and over. His reward isn't far off. That is where I must put my focus. All he has given in this fight has a reward. We, his family and friends, gather physically or in thought to continue prayers and love for him as he battles.

> Marcia- there is a quote that I've found comforting.
> "Do not look forward to what might happen tomorrow. The same everlasting Father who cares for you today will care for you tomorrow and every day. Either He will shield you from suffering, or He will give you unfailing strength to bear it. Be at peace then and put aside all anxious thoughts and imaginations."
>> — St. Francis De Sales
>> —Dawn

> Jim and I sit here this morning reading and sharing your eloquent words. Our words fail us right now, but the depth of our love for the two of you and power of the prayers we send on your behalf never fail or cease.
>> —Linda S

> No two people could have fought this horrible disease harder than you and Bill have. Prayers that the procedures and medications will leave Bill pain free and that God will hold you and your family very close today.
>> —Sue

Well, as the day began, this has turned out much better as just being in your own "space" will allow you to do and say what all are feeling in privacy and with no disruptions. At this time this is truly sacred space in every sense, as you face the choices that will be ahead and you can do so at whatever pace you all need. I know the draining of the fluid will provide some relief and as he feels not so physically uncomfortable all of you will feel that tiny bit also. This is a powerfully moving time for all involved. It seems maybe, even in his acceptance, as you seem to say, that he is again helping set the tone for this next leg of the journey that all of you are on in every sense of the word. If words and love and thoughts and prayers were tangible, the room would be filled and over flowing. Take care of one another, please, as you care for this remarkable person. Thanks for being so faithful and taking the time to keep us all in the loop.

—Louann

Sports Medicine

August 2, 2018

Bill's body is housing four less liters of fluid tonight. He has less pain because of the nerve block yesterday and a much more comfortable abdomen. My sister Amy and nephew Riley left last night for home. Niece Chelsea also left but her sister Cassie stayed. Nephews Jim and Bill came this morning for a brief time. The northern Michigan Wright clan headed home tearfully realizing that future good byes are uncertain. Bill's brother Sam and wife Cathy left for Grand Rapids. Tom took Bill's mom home and a quiet descended on the halls.

My sister Linda and our kids have been here today. Bill was more alert after his procedure making us chuckle with silly and incomplete thoughts. Most of the time we're stumped but then he will give us a charming grin. It's a bit of a puzzle anticipating the direction of the conversation but we do our best. He is without pain meds right now so we know much of this is how his body is responding to the dysfunction of critical organs.

We'd planned to go out for an early dinner together but Bill seemed sad as we prepared to leave, so I stayed with him. He ate a three inch square of pretty decent pizza. The nurses brought a warm blanket and we discovered a pre-season football game on TV! His eyes are glued to the screen and he seems as contented as I've seen him in quite a while. I've never thanked God for football—but tonight it's an answer to prayer. He's happy.

> *Take blessings wherever they may be found! Pizza and football, whatever helps.*
> *My heart aches for all of you who love Bill so dearly, and for all those whom he loves. My continual prayer is that peace, love, grace, and blessings enfold you all. take care.....*
>
> *—Pat S*
>
> *Pizza and football—it's worked for me for many years! Glad to hear Bill's pain has decreased and that you are so steadfast in your love and support for him. God has you in his care.*
>
> *—Don*

I'm so glad that Bill can still enjoy some simple everyday things like football and pizza that we just take for granted. I sincerely hope that the team he's rooting for wins. The fact that a sense of humor remains with both of you in this most difficult of all situations, says a lot about the wonder and resilience of the human spirit.

Praying for some rest for both of you tonight.

—Sue

Home

August 3, 2018

We are making plans for Bill to move to the Hospice House in our hometown this afternoon. He's fought so hard with his "Strong Will" but it's time for him to rest and be cared for in this lovely setting. An ambulance will transport us back to Adrian and as we settle in I'll post more. Please know the door is open should any of you wish to stop. Our love and gratitude for all of our "followers" is great. You are all part of this journey.

> *Oh how I wish in this earthly head of mine to see a different posting. But in my heavenly mind and heart, you are so blessed to soak up the time here and allow Bill to keep blessing others and doing God's kingdom work while here! Cannot wait for God to say to him "well done, good and faithful servant!" Love you both so much*
>
> *—Sally R*

> *All of this is because you have allowed us to be a part of this hard yet beautiful journey. Your commitment and love has shown thru in ways beyond the two of you. You have not only invited us but encouraged and allowed us to be on the Strong Will team. Kind of weird that the strong Will is not any of us but really him. Sounds like a special place and it is back to Adrian where it all began, the love between you two, the diagnosis, the leaving, returning, going again, and now home to settle in. Life really is a circle....*
>
> *—Louann*

> *I wish to share with you and Bill a few verses of **II Timothy, 4:7-8.(NIV)** The Apostle Paul is speaking of his impending death at the hands of the Roman government. He sends these words of comfort to his young friend, Pastor Timothy. "I have fought the good fight, I have finished the race, and I have kept the faith. Now there is in store for me the crown of righteousness which the Lord .....will award to me." This same future is waiting for every Christian. Bill can rejoice right along with St. Paul and all Christians at the joy waiting for him. Love to you both.*
>
> *—Kris*

We welcome you home with sad hearts. At the same time we thank you for sharing your journey with us. The eloquence of your posts have been nothing short of miraculous...such a gift and witness to us. God's mercy and compassionate grace will continue to follow you to our beautiful Hospice House. Peace and love to you all.

—Sally P

The Cocoon

August 3, 2018

After the flurry of arriving at Hospice House and settling in, we were treated to a wonderful dinner by dear friend, Joyce. Neighbors Bob and Cindy stopped— sharing love and beautiful flowers. They brought along daughter Katie and her adorable boys. Bill has been very quiet but he clearly greeted the little ones with, "How are you?" and a wave. Aaron, girlfriend Deb, and Jenn spent some time here too. Pastor Drew stopped by and lifting a beautiful prayer and later a priest came to anoint Bill.

Now it is quiet with just the two of us "breathing the same air." The sweetness of this moment isn't lost with me. How many more evenings will there be? I'm mysteriously finding contentment listening to his soft snore and feeling gratitude for the care he is getting. It is a terribly sad time. I wish it wasn't happening. I know we've done everything possible to find treatment. We sought doctors and clinics and highly skilled expertise. It just wasn't meant to be. And in the end, God will reveal His perfect plan. We, His servants, stand waiting.

> *All the research I'm sure you read and discussed, visiting other hospitals and getting other doctor opinions to help Bill kick the hideous cancer, I hope gives you relief in knowing you did all you could. I am sorry where you are at this point. May you, Bill and your family find some comfort that he is in the best place at this time. Hugs.*
>
> *—Nancy H*

> *Through your posts, it is shown the strength the Lord has given you and Bill through all of this. Praying for comfort for you and your families. Take care and hugs!!*
>
> *—Cherryl*

> *May there be peace for you and Bill. And may you be surrounded by love, blessings, and grace beyond measure. Thank you for continuing to share this journey. It is a rich gift to us all.*
>
> *—Pat*

> *Bill and Marcia-*
> *I hope you feel strength from God's strong arms holding you. He will get Bill to his next resting place where Bill will be comfortable and in no pain. Have faith as the journey unfolds. We're all sending love and prayers your way.*
>
> *—Joanie*

Finding Serenity

August 4, 2018

Over twenty-five visitors stopped to see Bill over the course of the day. So many dear, sweet friends and family were here— and on some level I'm sure he knew it. Dinner arrived and we again enjoyed the kindness. It's humbling to be the recipient of these gifts. It's much easier to be "doers" for others. But there is grieving and healing and so much love infused in these acts of kindness. We are grateful. I speak for Bill because I know he's sensing this "village" of support.

> *You do have a village surrounding you and Bill. Sorry we aren't closer this*
> *summer, but know that you both are in our thoughts and prayers.*
>
> *—Ginny*

> *We …..are keeping you close in prayers for comfort and peace. You have been*
> *such a strong, courageous woman, Marcia… and I thank you for continuing*
> *to share your journey with us. May you have a restful night.*
>
> *—Marcia L*

> *What a serene and peaceful place. What a blessing for Bill, you and all your*
> *friends who are able to visit and share their love for you. I'm sorry I couldn't*
> *be one to share my love in person. Sending prayers.*
>
> *—Diane*

> *Such a peaceful place.*
> *You are surrounded by love with those who walk by your side and those who*
> *walk with you in spirit.*
> *I'm so sorry Bill's end on earth has arrived. Know that you will continue to*
> *be loved and supported. May you ease through the next few days with Bill's*
> *spirit at your side.*
>
> *—Joanie*

Strong Will

As gently and softly as death can come, Bill slipped from us tonight. Around 10 PM the fireworks were exploding at a nearby festival signifying the end of the evening—but another end occurred simultaneously in a much more devastating way. Bill, our precious husband, father, brother, son, and friend to many— ended his fight with cancer and was wrapped in the loving arms of Jesus. This man who was so good and loved so deeply is free from the misery and pain—and for that I rejoice. His courage and beauty and overwhelming love for many will live within us forever. But right now, at this very moment, I cannot imagine life without him. I cannot feel him close to me anymore. I grieve the loss of a best friend, partner, and husband of unparalleled excellence. The future seems empty and lonely. I've always said Bill loved me the way I've always wanted to be loved. I hope I've done that for him. I hope he knew how much I loved him and how joyous our reunion will one day be— but tonight I cry in the hopelessness of profound loss.

> *No words can ease the pain of a loss as great as losing your best friend or your father. We can find a measure of comfort in Bill being pain free and wrapped in God's loving embrace. You will notice in the days and weeks to come he will be with you in a less tangible way but he will be with you in your heart as he always has been.*
> *My thoughts and prayers are with you all.*
>
> *—Claudia*

> *My heart goes out to you. I didn't know it would be so quick but you never have enough time anyway. Hang in there…. I know you have family to support you. Lean on them and get through the next couple days. You are loved.*
>
> *—Barbara*

> *Marcia and your whole family...you have loved, been loved, and shown God's love in ways that are simply to be praised. To know that your Bill, God's Bill, is forever home provides a strange peace during an earthly time that seems to feel very little peace. Know that the same God who welcomed Bill with amazing arms and a celebration beyond our imagination, is the same loving God who now promises to care for each of you. Accept and welcome the love of friends and family now... thank you for sharing Bill with all of us.*
>
> *—Sally R*

Oh my, as his trek has physically ended, his impact and profound, positive influence on so many will continue in both large and very small ways you will never know. Of course, who you and your family are, plus dear friends and countless others will be the real living legacy of who he was. We will all continue to carry on with the things learned by his example. That is no consolation for the unimaginable loss of just his not "being" physically there. Again, no idea of the pain and yet small joy of not seeing this man who was clearly loved by so many battle against such an insidious disease that could not be won on Mother Earth. Wishing some moments of quiet reflection and maybe smiles as you recall the magical story of you two...there would never be a right time for something this good to end but many of us are celebrating that the story happened. Peaceful thoughts and strength being sent your way.

—Louann

He knew and knows how much you love him and was humbled and filled with joy that you did and still do. That was one of the things that endeared him to us. He thought he was the luckiest man on earth to love so deeply and to be loved in return. He knew, Marcia. He knew. We send an extra measure of our love to you during this sorrowful time.

—Linda S

I think maybe death does not end love, but changes it. Sometimes it takes a very long time to figure out how all that works. May love, grace, and rich blessings surround you, all whom Bill loved, and all those who loved him. Thank you for sharing this sacred journey with us. Be at peace in whatever ways you can. Sending much love and continual prayers.

—Pat

Arrangements

August 6, 2018

The past two days have been busy in a numbing sort of way. My sister, Amy, has been here helping as we made decisions for Bill's funeral. She has been a rock helping me focus and make decisions and so has Jenn with her clear thinking and pragmatic suggestions. It's all quite surreal. As we go about the day it feels as if he's in the hospital or at an appointment and I'll see him any minute. That will take some reconciliation once everyone goes home and life continues. But for now, I'm grateful for Aaron, Jenn and Amy and their help.

The visitation is Friday, August 10 from 2-7 PM with a prayer service at 6:30 and an Irish toast at 7:00 PM.

Funeral service is Saturday, August 11 at 11 AM. Family will greet guests an hour before the service.

So now, we are working to create a service fitting this wonderful man with some personal touches that we hope he would like. It is a labor of love and I know at the end of the day I'll crave wanting to see what he thought about it all— to debrief all the little details we planned and get his reaction. I also know that won't happen. It will be a lonely feeling and one that I'll have to learn to adjust to going forward. But I can't help but feel I will "know" intrinsically how he feels. He will be with me...my sweet William, my Strong Will.

> *It's all too familiar. You are adjusting to the new normal It will get better but it doesn't go away.*
> *—Barb*

> *As Barb said you will be adjusting to a new normal. Bill's passing has brought back so many painful memories for me - I can actually say I know how you feel. You have so many friends and family for support which sadly, I was lacking. Please call on them when you need a support system, someone to talk to, it's all about you now and taking care of yourself and making a new path for yourself.*
> *—Luana*

> *Bill will be there in spirit. Whatever you plan, it will be to honor him and his mark that he's left on this world. Prayers that you will get through this with peace and comfort.*
> *—Sue R*

Preparations

August 8, 2018

Yesterday we met with our pastor to make decisions about the funeral service. It turned out to be a special reminiscing experience and that was comforting. People have provided meals and food with such generosity. That, too, means so much. Cooking and meal preparation is just overwhelming right now. Having these days between Bill's passing and the visitation has helped us collect ourselves. It has been a hectic two weeks. Sleep is elusive and I try to go to bed really tired. Last night we had a bonfire in our woods with Aaron, Jenn, my sister Amy, good friends and neighbors Bob, Cindy and their son Nate. We missed our Strong Will in person but his presence was among us as we engaged in a familiar and enjoyable time with loved ones. Later, as Aaron and Bob supervised the burning down of the logs, "Hotel California" began to play- its sound wafting through the night putting a smile on my face. Bill's very favorite song.

> *Hotel California has played three times on the radio while I've been in the car in the past week. His presence is definitely felt and strong.*
> —Mackenzie

> *Music is so powerful in our lives. Glad you are hearing familiar, sweet songs with good memories tucked into them. Although, I can't recommend checking into The Hotel California. How about a nice Best Western or Days Inn instead?*
> —Linda S

> *I am thankful for your continued writings, Marcia! We continue to keep you and your children in our prayers! Thinking of you today—with love!*
> —Nancy M

The Visitation

August 10, 2018

Today we held the visitation for Bill at the funeral home. It was a remarkable day- so *many* people stopped to share some time with us. It was humbling, sweet, and precious. There was a brief prayer service at the end with a toast beautifully led by Aaron. We drank to a very special man with a sip of Irish whiskey. A tribute fitting of a great man! Later, friends and family gathered in the backyard around another bon fire continuing toasts as we listened to music by the Eagles. What a dear and special night! Without question, this was such a fitting way to remember and treasure this wonderful man. His presence was felt. I know he was with us smiling and reveling in the joy of togetherness.

> *We were so happy to see you, your sisters, your children, and your friends.*
> *I must comment on the funeral home. In my experience, they tend to be*
> *dark and somber places. This was bright and warm with lots of windows.*
> *Or maybe it was all the beautiful sunflowers… and all the beautiful people*
> *gathered together for a common purpose: love, support and grieving together*
> *the loss of this special man. Love you, friend.*
>
> —*Linda S*

A Eulogy for Bill

August 12, 2018

The funeral was yesterday and it was a tribute I think Bill would have loved. Drew Hart, the pastor, wove a perfect collection of stories and scripture and prayer into the service. Friend and immensely talented Jillienne Bowers played "Amazing Grace" and "Danny Boy" on the violin. We sang "Be Thou My Vision" because Bill loved the traditional Irish melody and lyrics. As we recessed, *Hotel California* played—Bill's very favorite song and the one he proclaimed he wanted played at his funeral *many* years ago. So we did.

I spoke briefly about this man who has influenced so many and enriched my life in ways I never knew possible. This is what I said:

As fireworks lit up the sky on Saturday night, Bill Wright slipped from this world into the next— his eternal reward and home.

There is something about Bill.

He was a man who never understood his own worth. His goodness was steadfast and his love immense. He was complex—sometimes mistreated and sometimes misunderstood.

As a young man, he was a scholar athlete of the year. He was invited to West Point. He medaled in so many sports his letter wasn't visible. He scored the first touchdown in his high school's history. He worked summers and weekends as a bagger in a local grocery store but had a gift for numbers. When the cooks from the local summer camp came in to buy groceries, the cashier called Bill over not just to bag the food, he added in his head as she entered each purchase into the cash register calling out, "Ten cans of beans at twenty-nine cents,"etc. When the huge order was done, she would turn to Bill who gave her the total he'd mentally added in his head and it always matched her tape. He had that capacity to remember numbers so accurately! If you didn't have a pen to jot down a phone number, you had Bill.....I would say help me remember this number and he would. Sometimes months later he would say, "Can I let that number go now?" He'd hold it in his head till he got the OK to forget about it.

And he learned to build with his uncles. Our family adopted a phrase coined by his Uncle Earl. When something didn't fit just perfectly, Uncle Earl would say, "Oh well, that's why they make trim." We have used that expression adapting it in a variety of ways...... If something required a do over, we might say, "Oh well, that's why they make (whatever needed to be corrected.)

If a recipe flopped we might say, "Oh well, that's why they make restaurants...."

As an adult, he took those skills he learned in his youth to oversee the design and construction of three of his own homes... and two cabins.

He was brilliant with finance: figuring out complex projects like building the wide area network for school districts and municipalities, to creatively financing a state of the art football field with artificial turf. His lobbying in Lansing literally saved the existence of ISDs (service organizations supporting schools around Michigan) and received his second standing ovation at the school year's opening day with over 240 people in attendance.

He loved learning... economics, politics, finance, global issues, sports, beauty in art, nature, and life. He loved the quality of being succinct....when someone tended to pontificate you could sense his annoyance. Getting to the point mattered. I'm the opposite....happy to extoll his gifts. Boy! Would he be embarrassed right about now. He really was a Renaissance man—possessing a brilliance with immense compassion, amusing in ways that caught me off guard and made me laugh.

And he loved deeply.

He worried about me being alone. I worried about me being alone. But his example of unselfishness gave me courage. He protected those he loved with a great fierceness. His endearing and close relationship with his son Aaron was a hallmark of the immensity of his love. My own Jenn and Zac were recipients of that, too. Young people were drawn to him....nieces and nephews, friends of our own children....they loved Bill. He was the love of my life and I am so very blessed to have shared almost twenty two years with him. We just ran out of time.

He wanted to go to Ireland. We had just begun traveling in retirement—but ran out of time. He was learning to fly fish with his dear friend, Sherm—but ran out of time.

He wanted to see his first grandchild— but ran out of time.

He wanted to see the Lions win a super bowl—maybe that one is a little futile!

The day he got his diagnosis last fall, there was a brilliant sunrise. For several days it was clear and sunny and beautiful. I think that shed clarity on the path he would take. He began to gather his support team with family, friends, and clergy so he could talk and process what lay ahead. Pragmatic, poised, practical…. with amazing grace given the immensity of what was to come. He took risks. He tried and failed but continued to seek answers, solutions, and what became the unreachable cure. Never did I hear "Poor me." Never did he pity himself. He regretted the little time he felt he had. His zest for life and all he wanted to do was slipping away. In the end, he gathered his family….dispensed words of wisdom, humor, and silly random thoughts. But in those moments of uneven clarity, his truth shone through. We saw the man. The person who was cheated of so much life. We felt his love, his warmth, his fierce loyalty to others.

And I? I was the luckiest recipient of all. I was his wife. No sweeter words could be stated today for me. I was privileged to share many years with him and to be part of his journey right to this very day.

God Bless you, Bill Wright, my Strong Will. You have made me a better person because of your love.

> *Marcia, your words so beautifully describe Bill. I feel I know him well. You were truly blessed to have had him in your life although not as long as you both would have liked. I knew you before Bill, and know you to be a strong, loving gifted woman. Although being alone is not the path you would have chosen, you will continue to be that person. And you will always have Bill's spirit and love surrounding you. Love you.*
>
> *—Diane*

> *Oh, Marcia, this is so beautiful! I was in tears as I read this. You and Bill were truly blessed with a great love for each other. I am so happy you had each other, even if only for a short while. I pray that love and your memories will help to sustain you as you begin the next chapter of your life. Let God guide you through each day to whatever good things He has in store for you. Thank you for sharing this journey. May God comfort you and give you His peace as you step into this new stage of your life. Love and prayers and hugs,*
>
> *—Linda L*

Beautiful...Just beautiful words of Bill's life, the love you shared and God's love. Tears of so many emotions are being shared with you along with prayers for your journey. Daughter Kylee sang, "10,000 Reasons" (**song and lyrics by Matt Redman**) *with the worship band at church today and we thought of Strong Will's journey to Heaven. The chorus: "and on that day when my strength is failing, the end draws near and my time has come, still my soul will sing your praise unending, 10,000 years and then forevermore" reminded her of Bill. Peace, Joy, Blessings and Love.*

—Lisa D

Thank you for posting this. Jim and I read it together. We, who love each other deeply, want that kind of love to be experienced by those whom we love. When we met Bill, we knew that kind of deep love was possible for the two of you. We wanted that for you. We had prayed for that experience for you even before you met Bill. We are praising God today for the love you shared.

—Linda S

The First Day of Life Without Bill

August 13, 2018

Yesterday began a new chapter. Life without Bill. Family began to disperse after a beautiful brunch delivered by my P.E.O. sisters. Today Linda and Steve leave too. Aaron is here for a little while as he makes decisions about work. It will be nice to have the company and a little extra "noise" around the house. Over the past week people pitched in and helped with so many projects or tasks which was a great help. The boys installed new outside lights. My brother-in-law, Dan, repaired landscape lights that haven't worked for a long time. The kindnesses are many and I'm so grateful. As I move through the day I'm struck by how typical and atypical this is— all at the same time. I moved a trash can outside and felt this awful stab of sadness. Such a mundane task! Chatting with Zac as he packed to go home I burst into tears! I know this is "normal." I'm grieving. No one can make it better. All the love and caring is *so* appreciated, but in the end it's mine to adapt and get through.

Sometimes I feel ordinary. There is always a gnawing grip inside me, but distractions make that diminish. So now I have a strategy: stay busy, be active, and don't spend too much time thinking about it. My friends call it the new normal. Over time it will get better. On and on we identify or label this process with the realization that it's how this goes. I get that.

I just miss him.

> *Crazy how love sneaks up and bites us right in the heart huh! The tears are the healthiest part of your adjustment. Folks around you understand it, expect it and welcome your human side. So it is okay.............. just be you! Remember you will always "go there", and in time, day by day, moment by moment, you will find out you still "go there," but you don't "dwell there" as much. For now, love him, miss him, and remember with a smile through your tears how awesomely blessed your time was with him. Any time you get stuck, just say "Jesus," and He will provide a calm that nobody here can give you....*
> *Love and hugs on this new day. Hang tough! You are doing great!*
> *—Sally R*

A man like Bill deserves a lot of the good grieving, the bad grieving, and the ugly grieving. It turns out that all of it is good grieving. Don't ever be ashamed when your real feelings overwhelm you. All of your grief honors him and heals you.

—Linda S

So many of your friends and family wish that there was something we could do to make it better, but of course no one can. Grief is odd. I know someone in grief who cries brushing her teeth. Prayers that this will be an OK day for you to get through.

—Sue

Death for the Living

August 16, 2018

Death for the living is not all it's cracked up to be. Those of us who believe in life everlasting know that the physical separation caused by death is temporary. One day, we will be reunited with our loved ones who've gone before us. I'm finding that this fact is not comforting today. I'd like to sit and talk with Bill-before-cancer. I'd like to hug him or be waiting for him to get back from cycling. I'd like to think about what we'll have for dinner. I just want what I cannot have.

I went to the funeral home today with Jenn (bless her) to gather the memorials, thank you stationary, photos and the memorial DVD. That probably contributed to the pit in my stomach. Then I watched the DVD recalling some really happy times. A couple of friends stopped by to visit and tomorrow I'm going shopping and out to lunch with another friend. I read on the wonderful porch Bill had built for me, and it *rained* which I love! There is *some* normalcy here, you see? But then there is this *huge* blanket of sadness. It rises and falls in waves. A tsunami of emotions.

The "G" word.

I'm grieving.

And I don't like it one bit.

> *Marcia, Each day you swim through the sadness, you're one day closer to being out of it. I love how you continue to feel Bill's presence. You ARE inspiring!*
>
> —*Joanie*

> *Another "g word" is giving. That is what both of you did all the time to so many. So the grief is a given and know how many benefited from that word that bound you together. The fact you are on the porch he gave you seems to be an ongoing example of his giving and you enjoying that work of love. Not the same for sure and I know the days minus cancer and Bill the battler will be difficult to say the least. Just a day or minute and memory will be what will ensure that you are doing what he would like, minus the tears and heart so wounded.*
>
> —*Louann*

These are difficult emotions to handle. Pray for strength, wisdom and perseverance. You will need these as you slog through each day. One day you will realize you have forged a new normal but until then feel your feelings, your anger, your sadness, your need for normal. Let HIM know, HE will carry you.

—Claudia

I know how you feel Marcia. I talked to our friend, Rhea, this week and we all seem to be in the same sad boat. Some times are good and other times are downright depressing. Mine is easing a bit after 8 months (Really, it's been that long?!) but I still think he will walk through the door or I pick out what he would like for dinner when I go to the store. I gave some of his shirts to my brother-in-law and when I see him or pic of him with them on I remember how Keith loved that shirt or he wore that one out to dinner when we went somewhere. I have learned to embrace the lonely times and really enjoy the friends who have stood by. You will too - remember God loves you and is with you through it all.

—Luana

There is no other experience that is the same as losing a spouse especially one as young and vibrant as Bill. It's so unfair that his life got stopped in the middle before he had a chance to finish all that he wanted to do. It sounds like your heart aches for the ordinary things like hugs and dinner plans. All of us should cherish the ordinary things every day.

—Sue

The Impact of Comfort

August 19, 2018

There is a direct correlation between connection and comfort. People say, and it's incredibly well intended, "Let me know if there is anything I can do." I'm not sure those who are grieving know what they need from others to ease the grief. It's all such uncharted territory. But what I'm beginning to realize is that the deeper the relationship is with someone, its comfort is more impactful. It may be that it's an understood level of communication or connection but it's stronger in the "result zone". Without question, *all* efforts of comfort matter. I'd never discourage an attempt to reach out to someone who is hurting. It really does lift and strengthen the person who has lost someone—subtly, and over time. The realization comes in little snippets. ("That wasn't as hard" or "I can do this.") It's a process and a journey indeed. That continues without Bill physically by my side.

Last night I went out for dinner with dear friends Kathy and Dave. When our drinks arrived, we toasted to Bill. Over the years we've toasted to many events or occasions but there was no question in our hearts last night. We simply knew that would be the toast. And with our eyes glistening we smiled and said, "To Bill."

You continue to be the Giver, I am so glad you are continuing to share your thoughts with us. It helps us to understand this sad process and hopefully be supportive of you and others. Much love coming your way.

—*Diane*

Such words of wisdom and insight.

—*Lynne*

Through this journey, you have been a help to others. God Bless!

—*Ginny*

Good friends are the best!

—*Debbie B*

Marcia—thank you continuing to share! You continue to be in our prayers and we wonder how you are managing—so thank you for letting us know . Blessings to you –and with a prayer that today will be a little easier than yesterday. Much love to you!

—*Nancy M*

Learning to "Be"

August 20, 2018

Grief slows you down. For me, a person who is generally "go, go, go," I'm noticing that just before I get out of bed in the morning, I am slowed internally. I want to roll over and snuggle up against Bill, his sturdy body solid and strong. And when I can't, I think about it. I remember the feeling. It washes through me strangely absent physically—but imbedded in my memory and senses. I wonder if as time passes that it will be hard to pull that memory as intensely? I wonder will that fade away over time? I hope not. I hope I can always feel that connection. It's such a common thing. We take it for granted not giving it a thought. Until it's gone.

Bill's amazing surgeon in Milwaukee called last night to offer his condolences. He said he admired Bill's strength and assured me they are working hard to find a cure. I've said it before, but this is a very special man who is doing what he should be doing to help others. And one day, there *will* be a break through. How wonderful it would have been to be in that cohort! Imagine the thrill of being blessed with extended life! But for us, that did not happen. For us, we keep praying for that to be for others. And as for those sweet memories? We just cherish them. Every single day. Oh yes, we do!

> *The intensity of a presence of absence is so profound...on so many levels... but I truly believe you will remember. But hopefully the intensity will be more with the memory of his presence than the grief of his absence...love you dear sister*
>
> *—Linda, Marcia's sister*

> *I agree with Sue. After our granddaughter, Lily was born, her father, Steve, kept friends and family apprised of her condition (born at 24 weeks and one day, weighing in at 1 pound, 5 ounces) on a site provided by the March of Dimes. Finally she came home from the micro-preemie NICU at St. Joseph's Hospital. Four months later, Kelley had all of his posts printed and bound. It is such a precious document for our family. It reminds us of being held in prayer through the highs and lows of that time. Lily is now a happy, healthy 9 year old going into 4th grade. Someday that book will be hers.*
> *I encourage you to have your posts printed and bound. They will be a tangible memory of your journey through these past months. Please think about it, dear friend.*
>
> *—Linda S*

Your words are so eloquent and they just speak volumes. Several people have said that perhaps someday when you feel up to it that all of your Caring Bridge entries could maybe be put into book form to help others that are going through what you and Bill have gone through.

—Sue

Sharing this post with my mom, who has been learning a "new normal" since 2008 assured me, and wanted you to know—it truly does get easier. Not to say it does not remain tough during all the many, many layers of change....always searching for something, any little thing that is "routine," or "normal." When she finds it, she hangs onto to it. Her ability to stay in His word has brought her some of the most comfort with promises that we don't understand, but the Author of the Words we do know, and trust, and lean into. Just saying the name "Jesus" can change a moment, a mood, and a hurdle. That promise of comfort is sometimes our very best "normal!' Love and huge hugs...

—Sally R

A Keepsake

August 23, 2018

I've been wanting to hear Bill's voice and today I stumbled upon a voice mail message on my phone. He called when I was out running errands and was worried because it took me longer than what I thought. I was so elated to hear him and I listened to the message over and over and sobbed. Ironically, he ended the message with "Love to see you, Babe."

Me too, honey. Me too.

I'm so glad you found this!

—Sue

He will always be with you and sometimes in very unexpected and wonderful ways, like today. You know the message then is the same as it is today. From his heart to yours.

—Louann

I thought for some reason, when Bill passed, that you would discontinue posting on Caring Bridge©. I am thrilled that you would allow us to continue the journey with you as you grieve and find your way to living life without Bill being here on earth. I think of you every day. I was reading about George Burns and Gracie Allen and their deep love for each other. He said, that after her death, he was devastated and bereft. One night, he decided to sleep on her side of their bed. He thought, "If I sleep in her place, then her place isn't empty." It gave him comfort to sleep where she had slept for so many years. I am learning so many things about losing the great love of one's life. Thank you for sharing this painful and difficult time. You are forever the consummate teacher. I love you for this and for so many other reasons.

—Linda S

A Gift that Keeps on Giving

August 24, 2018

This is my first week end home *alone*. Aaron and Jenn have done a great job of making sure I have companionship, but this week end they both have things to do—as they should. I'm tucked in with a glass of wine, Netflix, and the only thing that would make it any better would be to be "breathing that same air" with Bill. But, right now, in this little moment, I am fairly content.

Today Bill's car became *my* car and his Mustang gained a new owner per Bill's instructions: Aaron. Little by little Bill becomes more a part of us. His generous spirit continues to bestow gifts.

> *Continue to hang on to the many memories and move forward.*
> —*Ginny*

> *Hugs my dear........... it's all part of the journey.*
> —*Cindy H*

> *Marcia, you are so modest in so many ways but we all know of Bill's and your generosity— and willingness to be such a part of making his wishes happen— might not occur if it were not for your love of him to make sure all of that occurs. You are the one that is "here" and so keeping him alive in so many ways. Hard as it may be, you continue to show us the outward signs of the inward feelings.*
> —*Louann*

Wrapped in Warmth

August 27, 2018

My friend, Jan, knitted a scarf and gave it to me today. She started knitting it when Bill was first diagnosed. The colors are vibrant and rich and it will be a perfect addition to my winter coat. I'm struck by the symbolism: not only is it a very special gift, the purpose is symbolic of Bill. His love for me, constant warmth and the way he wrapped his arms around me will be imbedded in this lovely fabric. I can't think of a more perfect gift as I anticipate winter without Strong Will.

But wait! His angels are tending to me and I'm filled with gratitude on many levels.

> *What an incredible gift, made and given with love, and for sure received with love and gratitude . The symbolism of how so many things can be knitted together, if you look for the good and incorporate into your life, you are a master of that, dear friend.*
>
> *—Louann*

> *I love the colors. So rich. And you are rich in friends and family.*
>
> *—Linda S*

Learning to Live

August 30, 2018

As the "holiday" weekend approaches, I will be alone. It's not sad. I'm not afraid and I have things to do. Jenn and I may go to a movie or shopping. What I'm thinking about is the shift in living—now. In the past on Labor Day week end, we inevitably found ourselves doing some yard/home task we'd put off and finally decided to get it done. Bill would grump, "Everyone is having fun but us." And it was our own doing! Last year we spent Labor Day staining the deck on the cabin Bill and his brother owned. It was hot, hard work but we worked well together and it really looked great when we finished. We showered and went out for some dinner. Later we relaxed back at the cabin listening to music and marveling at how much we'd accomplished. Little did we know that a month later, Bill would have that terrifying diagnosis. He wasn't feeling well and hadn't for some time, but he pushed himself to wrap up that job before the weather turned cold. When Bill Wright decided to get something done, he did. As I sit here tonight pondering that little vignette in our memorable history, I smile. Tears flow remembering, wishing I could turn back the clock, change the course of time, and have just a little more time. Yet, in all of this immense sadness there is this: nothing can erode or destroy a memory. It is within us always. There may be grieving but that is the price of loving richly and well.

I wouldn't want it any other way.

> *Here you are, teaching us again. Jim and I read this together. We know that when "one of us is gone and one is left behind to carry on", that "remembering will have to do; our memories alone will see us through." The memories will be sweet and sad, and good, bad and ugly, and to quote you, my dear friend, "that is the price of loving richly and well." It is a price either one of us will gladly pay when that time comes. As Garth Brooks sings in one of our favorite songs, "I could have missed the pain, but I'd have had to miss the dance." We are thrilled that Bill and you didn't miss The Dance. We wouldn't want it any other way either. Sending our love to you tonight, teacher.*
>
> *—Linda S*

I am so taken by your ability to pick through the junk and find the treasures that are so well hidden. Not many would be able to do that and, upon discovering, in this case a memory, dig it out and wipe it off and go right back to where you were. Forgotten memories are there and what an "ah ha" moment when you stumble on them and can make the love come vividly alive. Labor Day and your labor of love with keeping Bill right there seems like an OK spot for right now.

—Louann

The Measure of a Heartbeat

September 4, 2018

In a heartbeat life can change forever.

That relative measure of time says it all. Today marks the one month anniversary of Bill's passing. His entry into glory left us bereft, and as I ponder that it seems like it was only a heartbeat ago. In the same breath, it seems like *forever*. Sometimes I just call out Bill's name-as if I'm going to ask or tell him something. The ease of it on my tongue feels lovely, reassuring, and familiar. I know he won't answer. It's my silly way of keeping him present.

Tonight, Aaron, Jenn and I are going out to dinner together and we will raise a glass to Bill as we commemorate this first "milestone" and break bread together. But today, while the sun shines and the heat of summer lingers, I'm determined to show some random acts of kindness toward others. It gives a happy purpose to the day and honors a wonderful man whose kindness lived quietly in his soul.

> *Well, dear friend, taking time to continue to include all of us in this trip, is a whole lot of random kindness to so many in my book! Glad to be one of the recipients. Maybe even raise a toast to Bill for drawing so many of us together, and more importantly, for you keeping us together.*
>
> *—Louann*

> *I so appreciate your including all of us on your journey, Marcia. I know it must be difficult for you, but your words are helping others. I agree that your words are "random acts of kindness." Think of you so often.*
>
> *—Linda L*

> *Awesome to have made it a month. Your tender comments are heart-stopping. Thanks for sharing them.*
>
> *—Joanie R*

> *Thank you, Marcia, for sharing your life with us. The concept of time is such an elusive phenomenon. Happy times go by so quickly. A nice reminder to savor those moments. Love the way you are thinking of others as you move through this painful time. I believe that is the best way to heal. Sending love your way.*
>
> *—Diane*

Marcia,

I observed so many random acts of kindness performed by you in my nineteen years of our friendship. It is fitting that you are continuing to do that as part of Bill's legacy.

—Don

For Now

September 9, 2018

While Caring Bridge© is typically a site for loved ones to track progress for friends or family, it's become a forum of sorts for me and those who follow it. As I've said before there is a marvelous faith conversation from those of you who comment. Isn't that a wonderful way to share love and compassion?

As I fumble along this grief path, I continue to be humbled and feel such gratitude for those who've reached out through cards, calls, invitations to dinner or outings. When you know someone who suffers a loss and you want to do "something", consider that simple list. My wise friend and neighbor, Karen, lost her very young husband a couple of years ago. She was one of the first to stop with cookies (Who doesn't love cookies?) and said "Don't become a recluse. Get out there. Say yes to every invitation." She is right. These things help with loneliness and the immense loss.

This week I am driving to Chicago to see my sister and brother-in-law. Linda and I are flying to Atlanta for a couple of days. I'm *so* looking forward to the change of scenery and the wonderful companionship. I think I will need to keep spacing out these "buoys" as Bill called them. They give me reasons to look forward to the days ahead. This useful strategy is pretty simple but it works!

> *I'm so glad you're getting away and to spend time with your sister. You've done so much "hard" time in the past year. Here's to enjoying some easier time.*
>
> *—Sue R*

> *Good strategy, like the idea of buoys.. Safe, smooth travels.*
>
> *—Julie S*

> *Sister time is the best!!*
> *Thank you once again for keeping us all in the fold as our hearts journey with you. Here's to some simple joy as you keep moving forward.*
>
> *—Lynne*

Checking In

September 19, 2018

It's been a week and as I look back, it's a "work in progress". Time with my sister and family was priceless. Visiting Atlanta was a great distraction. It's a place I've never visited *with* Bill so there wasn't the memory of things *we* did, etc. It was a clean slate— new vistas and lots of fun. There were moments when I felt normal. I even slept reasonably well at night. This tells me that it will come. In time. There will be a new normal. There will be days of happiness and peacefulness. Maybe not now. Maybe not yet. But I do believe one day I will feel somewhat whole in a new way. That "glimpse" gives me hope. I can keep going. I can get up each day and face life without Bill. Sadly. Not as I wanted it to be, but I can do it. He would want this for me. I feel that strength from him. As much as we'd hoped for more time together, I feel him urging me along— a "super power of love" keeping me on the path. When we've loved so deeply, we want to honor these very special people in a manner that is fitting. We strive for grace and beauty and all things lovely that exemplify the relationship. Such bittersweet work!

> *It's not easy. One day at a time. Just keep pushing to get up each morning. I have no doubt you honor your love for Bill everyday just being you. You are an amazing person.*
>
> *—Marla*

> *Marcia - I was so glad you "checked in" and that you had such a nice get away with family and friends. It is good medicine. Take care. Hugs!!*
>
> *—Cherryl*

> *I am so proud of you big sister! You continue to amaze me and show the world the power of love well lived.*
>
> *—Amy, Marcia's sister*

> *Your reflections are so very insightful. Admire your spirit and pray for your continued healing through this saddest, hardest transition. Blessings.*
>
> *—Julie S*

> *I like that you said, "feeling somewhat whole in a new way" because that is what it is. Glad you are back.*
>
> *—Barbara*

You were always a strong woman: strong in your faith and your ability to love people. Bill's love made you even stronger. Your love for each other demonstrates even today and all the tomorrows you have the power and depth of love. We are all learning from you, teacher. We are learning from you as you share this new phase of your life and we are learning it from the artistry of your words. Our love for you grows as you reveal yourself in honesty. Thank you for your courage.

—Linda S

Such a powerful message & so much love for past, present & future.

—Steve & Carol

Falling Off the Throne

September 23, 2018

Sometimes what we know gets turned upside down. I've watched a certain TV evangelist for a long time. He has very positive messages about faith. Today, while dressing for church, his message unnerved me. The topic was "staying centered on God's throne." One of his examples included this thought: If we face a serious disease, being strongly centered on God's throne is more powerful than cancer. What?! Did we fall <u>short</u> in our faith walk during Bill's illness? That's not what I understood. Spiritual growth is hard. We do the very best we can. Christ lives in us. Challenges that come our way are not a result of God punishing us for a wrongdoing— or so I thought. Yet, the TV pastor gave the impression that underperforming in our Christian conduct (not being centered on God's throne) translates to: that's why there wasn't a cure, a miracle, a "fix."

I believe in things unseen. I try (sometimes unsuccessfully) not to lose faith, but what I heard today told me I wasn't steadfast enough. I didn't "do it right." For those of us struggling to make sense of loss, it's perplexing and hurtful. The God I know and love hasn't led me to this precipice. The God I know and love gave His Son to die for us— people who are fallible, broken, but earnestly striving to live in His example of love. It's all any of us can do.

> *Oh dear me, please remember you did everything just right for the deep faith you and Bill shared. While this message was unnerving to say the least, please remember it came from a human being. All of us see things differently at different times. It seems this may be a time when he was "just human" with all the frailties and mistakes we all make. Before we are anything else we are human. I'm sad this hit you at such a vulnerable time. Try to remember it was the human talking and not the God you know and trust.*
> *—Louann*

> *I think that the truth is that we all come to the end of this life and go on to something more eternal. I have no idea why some suffer greatly like Bill and that some slip away peacefully. I don't think that what we do or don't do has any effect on how or when we go. The number of our days is set before we are even born.*
> *—Sue*

I wholeheartedly disagree with that message. Yes, we are supposed to focus on God during times of stress and need. Do we come up short? Yes! We are human. Not being cured is not a punishment for falling short. The reason for the focus is that we may lean unto our Lord in times of great joy (a cure or healing) and in times of great sadness. He is our rock! He is our shelter! He is our stronghold and our sure defense, He will be our savior!

—Claudia

It is so unbelievably hard and unbearable at times to lose the love of your life. During those days something someone says can catch you off base and send you on a whirlwind of confusion. When that happens lean on God and allow Him to continue the process of healing your broken heart. "He heals the broken-hearted and binds up their wounds" **Psalm 147:3 (NIV)** *God promises to be with you and get you through this time of intense disappointment. "So do not fear for I am with you; do not be dismayed, for I am your God. I will strengthen you and help you, I will uphold you with my... hand."* **Isaiah 41:10 (NIV).** *Your Caring Bridge© friends are also here for you and we will continue to pray and love you dearly.*

—Lisa D

We can thank or blame Adam and Eve for sin and disease and death entering the perfect world God created. He created us with the ability to choose because He didn't want us to be puppets or robots or automatons. When they chose unwisely, and allowed evil to enter that perfect world, He then created a way for us to be redeemed and serve and love and praise Him. Both you and Bill chose wisely. Disease is NEVER a punishment. It happens in this imperfect world. I know that God held you both in His arms of love and wept with you as you wept. I am furious that this human made you doubt your faith or Bill's faith. Next week watch cartoons or the test pattern or reruns of I Love Lucy or leave the TV off. So there.

—Linda S

Reaping What You Sow

September 24, 2018

On Saturday, the local Rotary club sponsored a bike ride. Our friend, Rita, rode in honor of Bill. She has been our yoga instructor but she and Bill often cycled together on the Kiwanis trail. Part way into the ride they stopped, did yoga stretches, and along the way, they discussed some of the world's problems. Rita stated that after Bill died she wanted to do this for him. It was a beautiful tribute from a very special woman. It made me think about gifts that "keep on giving"- acts like this say two things: They speak to the kindness of those who demonstrate caring. And that, in turn, honors a wonderful man who loved and cared deeply for others.

Lovely...he lives on....

—Cindy H

Bill will always live on in my memory, especially the Christmas lights tour we took together many years ago! Love you.

—Dianna

The Slippery Slope of Grief

October 3, 2018

Time doesn't figure into this grief journey. Time is a measurement, a defined allotment on a clock or calendar or when a scheduled appointment takes place. I live in suspended time now, conducting my life in seemingly normal ways while feeling anything but that.

Tomorrow it will be two months since Bill passed away and I feel the worst today. I'm weepy, angry, overwhelmed, and so tired. Paperwork continues to mount. One stack is handled and another surfaces. I want to put all of that behind me. I want to focus on healing and being present in a peaceful moment. I want to renew a connection with God because it's frazzled. In my grief group we talked about anger, blame and accepting God's plan as sovereign. We've prayed for healing, the wisdom of doctors, and a miraculous cure. But in the end He knows the number of our days. And that stymies me. Why pray? If this is all decided long before we can possibly know, I know my prayers wanted something different than what God planned. And that's hard for me to accept. Grief, fatigue, mounting tasks and responsibilities come at me stabbing at my fragility. Tonight I'm weary. Hopefully in the days ahead this will ease. I can only hope.

Marcia, please know many are praying for you during this hard time. It is not easy and, even with time, there are sad days. I do know the Lord will never leave us and always hears our prayers. He has a path where He is leading us. It is for our good so we will see our loved ones again. Take care and hugs!!

—Cherryl

"Faith is the breakthrough into the depths of the soul that accepts the paradox with humility." Marcia, this is a quote from a meditation I read some time ago and I think it describes your journey. You are in the depths of your soul. Why is this pain part of your life if God loves you? It makes no earthly sense to me either. May you find strength, love and faith today in your journey. You are in my prayers.

—Diane

Prayers for rest for you! You sound exhausted. I think that people pray for all kinds of reasons. Some of those being for strength, comfort and feeling close to God.

—Sue

Your anger is powerful and justified and normal. But please don't let it separate you from the love and compassion from friends and relatives who continue their love and support and prayers for you. We are humbled that you share your soul with us. Your honesty helps us understand and guides our prayers for you.

—Linda S

A Voice Now Silent

October 14, 2018

Unless it's a recording, Bill's voice is silent. But despite this "silence" he still speaks in different ways. I feel him. I sense him. I miss him. I drove to see some of Bill's family in northern Michigan for a few days. The fall color was stunning and then I realized it was the first time I traveled on that highway without him to remark on the color, the beauty, and I bawled. I felt him, though. I know on some level he was with me and the time with his family was heartwarming and healing.

Today, Bill "spoke" again to my brother-in-law, Steven, as he watched his beloved Chicago Bears play football. He was missing the text bantering they engaged in—occasionally—so as not to disturb the plays.

He "talked" to his friend, Sherm as he dressed in a jacket for church. Sherm smiled recalling it as one Bill liked and commented on when he wore it.

Bill's voice is silent—yes, to our ears. But in our hearts he lives and continues to be a part of us in so many little ways-and that is more precious knowing we feel him from within us now.

The voice is silent.

The body no more.

But the love he shared is forever.

> *Silence is golden and so is your "Bill."*
>
> —*Dawn*

> *Bill speaks to us with our new furry addition to the family as I know Uncle Bill would have loved his name... maybe even call him "Rueben" to tease me.*
> —*Mackenzie (niece)*

> *Marcia, your words are profound and moving. You are correct that Bill's voice can and will continue to be heard in many hearts.*
>
> —*Diane*

> *The voices in our hearts and minds are sweet and precious. Your beautiful writing makes us better, Marcia.*
>
> —*Julie S*

Lighting a Different Candle

October 23, 2018

Tomorrow will be my first birthday without Bill- just one of many "firsts". I found the card he gave me last year where he wrote he was going to fight this cancer so we could have more time together. Oh, how he did! He tried so hard. I really thought he would be here longer than he was. I've felt sad all day and realize that's why. We become more acutely aware as we move through the days without our loved one. Life can get pretty close to normal and then there is an event or occasion that was so wonderful to share with them. But you can't. It's done. That has ended and you come face to face with yet another "adjustment." I'm grateful for the birthdays we *did* share—but it's never enough, is it?

> *I know just how you feel, Marcia. I have been though the first birthday, the wedding anniversary, now the holidays loom ahead and I am not looking forward to them. Keith passed the day after Christmas and was unresponsive for three days before that so I don't know how Christmas will look for me this year. It was so nice to see you yesterday. You always exude a positive spirit and it helps all of us who come in contact with you. Hope you can find some joy in your birthday and I wish you a birthday filled with peace and the knowledge that Bill loved you very much.*
>
> *—Luana*

> *It's a roller coaster.*
> *I'm so proud of how strong you are.*
> *May your birthday be filled with happy memories too*
>
> *—Joanie*

> *You have summed it up so well. All the firsts are so hard. I wouldn't have made it through without faith, family and friends. Praying for you on this journey we didn't want to be on.*
>
> *—Linda W*

Grief Ambush

October 29, 2018

As a breast cancer survivor, I have annual checkups with my oncologist who was also Bill's Michigan oncologist. It's been several months since I've driven that familiar route for Bill's chemo and various treatments— but today's trip caught me off guard. In grief group it's called a grief ambush— we can't see it coming. I was so sad and emotional recalling those drives in the late fall and winter earlier this very year. I puddled up during my lab work. I burst into tears when the PA came in to see me. When Dr. Margolis arrived he immediately said, "What's wrong?" I was really crying by then. Each of these care providers has a history: first with Jenn five years ago, with me four years ago, and finally with Bill. Such an intimate connection to us collectively— hoping, healing, and hanging on through huge and sometimes insurmountable odds. I was comforted by the compassion of this wise and dedicated staff of medical professionals who in the end just want to make cancer go away and restore health to many who aren't as lucky as Jenn and I are. Gabby, another PA, stepped in the room to say hello and sat with me as if it was all she had to do. We talked fondly about Bill—his strength and determination and how really awful pancreatic cancer is.

I guess today was another hurdle. Next year it will be easier. Before heading home I went to the hotel where we stayed after Bill's chemo treatments and had lunch with the woman who arranged for our hotel suite when we stayed there. She has become a friend. That's what's important to remember. In all of this sadness, there are angels and kindnesses that lighten our burdens.

> *Grief ambush—a perfect description of a real event. Sometimes I am just a mess. I hear a song on the radio and think of my mom and start crying because I still miss her. One time I was at a nursery and started crying and didn't know why. I finally determined that the smell of all the geraniums took me back to my Grandma's front porch. I have many happy memories from her house. These events aren't necessarily bad. Sometimes they are comforting - pleasant reminders of precious times. The one you just had was pretty raw. I am so thankful there were familiar folks there to share your memories and comfort you or grieve with you. Thanks for sharing this, dear friend.*
>
> *—Linda S*

So thankful to know you were surrounded by compassionate people through this grief ambush. May it always be so. Take good care, Marcia.

—Julie S

Thank you for sharing this painful, but meaningful day. You helped me understand those times when I have been grief ambushed. They are so painful, yet as Linda said, can be beautiful reminders for us. For you, not yet, but hopefully soon. Love you, Marcia. You are amazing.

—Diane

The "Soul" Phone

November 2, 2018

Today I deactivated Bill's cell phone. I grieved. Another link to life here on earth. As I looked over the apps he had on his phone, I saw the man Bill was: apps to pursue knowledge, news, financial references, current sports stats and first names of various writers he followed, texts to siblings, to me, to Aaron, Zac, and Jenn (who texted to him just two days before he died: "Get some rest"). Each piece we sever releases these earthly connections in a way that is profoundly sad. As these strands of life as *we* know it are cast aside, we know more concretely he is gone. From here. From what we know. He *is* in a place of glory. We long to be connected; yet it's not our time. We who are left to ponder these things are bereft. I weep for all that I no longer have. Yet, in this terrible time I seek comfort not only from my earthly angels who call, spend time with me, and connect in many ways, I look for God to lead me through the "shadow of death" and help me find comfort, peace, and hope in tomorrow.

What a difficult thing to do! We are all so connected through our phones these days. They are an extension of ourselves and are a datebook, a planner and a diary as we share with others. I'm so sorry you had to do this. Prayers that today will be a good day!

—*Sue*

That must have been a hard one. For some things I'd wish they'd stop or go away so I didn't have to take any action.

—*Cindy H*

Tangible reminders of Bill must be so bittersweet. My prayers continue for you.

—*Don*

You will come through the darkness. Peace be with you.

—*Ginny*

Hugs Marcia. I still have our friend, Dennis' messages on my phone. Since his passing, I sometimes I reread his messages and …debate whether to delete them.

—*Nancy H*

All Saints Day

November 4, 2018

Each year at church, there is a ceremony honoring people who passed away during the year. It's a very moving tribute but of course, this year was much more significant because Bill was being remembered. Twenty candles were placed on the altar –one for each person. As each name was read, his or her photo projected on the wall and a bell tolled for them. Family members lit a candle for their loved one. It was very somber and touching. I didn't want to light the candle alone at the early service (Jenn came to the later service where the ceremony was repeated). When I shared this at grief group this past week, one of my new friends said, "I'll stand with you. You shouldn't be alone." What a kind and loving act! She, too, grieves the very recent loss of her husband— but found strength to support me. On this third month "anniversary" day, I am blessed by the people God places in my life to offer comfort and prove His steadfast love is present. I give thanks for this, knowing Bill's love is within me. There is no penetrating darkness when there is Light.

I'm so glad you were able to have someone with you for both services. Your friend was correct in saying that you shouldn't be alone in your grief.

—Sue

What an incredibly thoughtful way to honor these people. The candles represent along with those who are there to actively participate, another milestone as it were.

—Louann

Another beautiful way to remember and honor those we love. Our church also does this and it is always a moving experience and a heartfelt reminder of those we have loved. I believe our loved ones are close to us— we can feel them in our hearts. This ceremony always helps me to do that. I'm sure Bill was smiling as he watched you light his candle with Jenn and the loving support of friends. We are all amazed at your strength and love.

—Diane

Getting Through the Holidays 101

November 11, 2018

Tonight the grief group topic covered strategies for coping with the holidays. We're all women. Most of us have lost our husbands. We've had good marriages and much for which to be thankful— but we're headed into a mine field of emotional trauma. Thanksgiving is almost here and Christmas will follow. New Year's Eve is our wedding anniversary which I'll need to face. These sessions are always insightful and offer practical ways to cope. It's faith based and we are reminded that while grief comes from the broken world in which we live, God is our source of comfort and strength. It's OK to "unleash" rage and sadness on His huge and loving heart. That's a reminder we all need as we travel this lonely path. But here's the other thing that keeps surfacing over and over: the support we give each other offers a unique level of understanding. We *know* the immense sadness of our fellow grief group members. We share stories and tears in the depths of this awful, awful journey. It's comforting. There is an invisible bond that I suspect will exist a long time for all of us. We are grieving in our own individual way but we are now all "wounded healers." We know the pain but we also comfort each other.

I would not have known the power of healing had I not been where I am today. Right now, I'm fragile. I'm broken. I'm managing. Some days I'm even okay. But I also know that in time it will get better. In time life will settle into a new normal. I'll *always* cherish the many memories and moments. I'll hold Bill in my heart with love, incredible gratitude, and always with the wistful hope that we could have had more time together. But tonight I'm grateful for the special bonds we've developed in this undesired sisterhood and the strength that comes from knowing one another.

Gratitude.
Yes.
And that's enough.

> *So glad you have one another that have the jagged broken heart you all share. It is a bond that words cannot describe, for sure, but it is your common denominator.*
>
> *—Louann*

Your post brought tears of love and hope for you in these next few weeks. You are both strong and weak, finding some strength in shared experiences. This is good.

—Linda S

Your post that I read this morning brought some clarity into my life. You had hope! Hope that Bill could and would recover after moving to another state, getting the best doctors in that field, and unsurpassed care. Then after what seemed hopeful, your hopes were dashed once his cancer metastasized. I didn't have any hope. Five years ago my husband, Keith, was diagnosed with Lewy Body Dementia— and from then on we knew there was no specialist, no hope. I have had five years to adjust to him dying, looking at him and being so sad not knowing how many days we would have together. If he hadn't fallen and broken his neck we may have had a few more "good" days. You are not only grieving the loss of Bill you are grieving the loss of your hopes and dreams being gone... You don't need to be strong all the time, there are memories to cherish and new memories to make.

—Luana

I'm so glad that you have this support group of other people who know, "how it is." You are so right about the holidays being a mine field. They are a celebration of family and your heart can't help but break when the one you love isn't there in body. It's especially difficult when your grief is so raw and new. Both of my parents have been gone for many years, but I never miss them more than at the holidays. My dad died at Thanksgiving and my mom on New Year's Eve. Prayers for you that you will get through these coming days ok.

—Sue

The Gift of Friendship

November 19, 2018

Bill and his friend, Marv went to a University of Michigan football game each year. Bill happily set aside his Spartan green and white to enjoy the camaraderie in this famous stadium. Each year he told Marv, "I'd love to bring Marcia. She's never been to the Big House." I didn't know that, but Marv remembered and he texted me hoping to make that wish a reality in honor of Bill. Would I like tickets to the next game? I read that message on my phone in the parking lot at Lowe's and burst into tears. What a generous offer! What a thoughtful tribute to Bill! So, on Saturday I went to the Big House with my son Zac, who is also a Michigan fan and it was a wonderful experience. I marvel at this touching gesture from a special friend. Strong Will's love flows through his generous earthly angels.

More gratitude.

> *What a kind and thoughtful gesture.*
> *Hope there was some Spartan love there as well!*
> *—Joanie*

> *This just thrills my heart: not just as a Michigan Alumna, but as another example of the love of friends towards such a man of worth: Bill. It is love in pure form. And of course, I am hoping that your experience in The Big House converted you to rooting for the maize and blue. Oh, rats. I realize that your heart for Bill would never let that happen. Let's just praise God for this wonderful demonstration of His love working in the hearts and minds of ordinary people.*
> *—Linda S*

Thankful

November 25, 2018

As the Thanksgiving weekend draws to a close I'm thankful for the many blessings in my life: loved ones with whom I share my life, for those who may not be with me now, but always in my heart. This is an important distinction— we can love and cherish even when those we love aren't present physically. That in itself is a gift.

These "first" holidays are hard— we miss the people we've shared these times with. The new normal begins without them. It's sad. Bittersweet. We gaze around the room filled with laughter and the aroma of wonderful food. Blessings and immense absences. He is not here. I'm beginning to know this strange but familiar sensation. Realization. Awareness. Breathing in and tasting the grief. Exhaling and releasing the anguish. The release is what we work hard to achieve.

I spent some time getting Christmas decorations out today. Each box reminded me of last year. As I packed up and put things away, I remember wondering what next year would bring, never truly thinking Bill would be gone. A needlework pillow with the design of a car loaded with a Christmas tree was a favorite of Bill's. I cried. It brought back the memory of buying it and enjoying its loveliness. Again and again that scenario played out with so many beautiful things. Giving ourselves permission to feel these moments of adjustment is part of this process. It's hard, but it's what we must do. I've known such joy and completeness. Grief follows when this is lost and in the end, I'm thankful.

> *You express your thoughts so beautifully, Your awareness and appreciation for the love that surrounds you, in spite of the pain, feels like grace to me. Bill is smiling on you and continuing to send his love. Sending you prayers and love.*
>
> *—Diane*

> *Thanks for posting this. We were thinking of you this weekend. Our kids were asking about you.*
>
> *—Linda S*

Lights of Love

December 2, 2018

The annual tree lighting at Hospice House is a lovely ceremony honoring loved ones. Each name is read and those in attendance join in singing Silent Night. The simplicity is perfect. Everyone shares a bond of love and sorrow for what is gone. Tonight, Aaron, Jenn and I attended to remember Bill: husband, father, and stepfather. What peace there was in being together. In that moment, on a soft and mild pre-winter night, we paused to let all that we felt waft around our loved ones in the spirit of unity. They were so loved— and we grieve.

> *We just came from a "Love Feast" Service. While sitting there listening to the choir sing Christmas carols and the lighting of candles held by about 2500 people, my thoughts turned to you and Bill and the tough journey you traveled together out of hope and love. May God bless you as you go through the holiday season and give you strength and love!*
>
> *—Dianna*

> *A beautiful gathering—full of love for those we grieve.*
>
> *—Julie S*

> *Peace and blessings to you!*
>
> *—Sue*

No More Roses

December 4, 2018

Bill has been gone four months today. I write these words and the grief swells up within me. How can it be? The days are normal and abnormal at the same time. It's Advent. The house is decorated as always looking the same as other Christmases. Cards are in the mail— with some addressed to my new grief group friends. (That is a positive— knowing these kindred women who share in this sad sisterhood.) My shopping is done and I'll wrap gifts soon—but nothing will be under the tree for Bill. I made fudge for the landscape crew but when I finished it, Bill wasn't there to say "I have to sample just a little. Your fudge is so good!" Those are the everyday differences that grip me. Simple. Maybe even petty. It is just such a change.

Today also marks the 26th anniversary of my mom's untimely passing. She was 64 years old and cancer took her, too. Each year, Bill gave me a red rose in her memory. Last year, as miserable as he felt, he arranged for a rose to be delivered. Such kindness and love!

But now there are no more roses.

> *I was thinking about you today knowing that it would be a difficult one (as they all are). Your much loved mom passed away just a few weeks before mine. We will soon be marking 26 years also. Time may make grief more bearable, but certainly not "easier." Prayers for you this day.*
>
> *—Sue*

> *Such beautiful, positive memories. Heart-warming and heart-breaking all at the same time. Take care, friend.*
>
> *—Julie S*

> *This is such a sad time for you. You have so many memories both loving and sad. Praying for you.*
> *A memory I have of you: I put the ornament you made for me over 40 years ago on my tree. It is still beautiful and always makes me smile as it brings with it memories of you.*
>
> *—Diane*

A Precious Addendum

December 5, 2018

I shared the story about the rose from Bill to honor my mom at Grief Share©. Unbeknownst to me, they decided this year could not go without a rose to commemorate the day and gave me a beautiful long stemmed rose.

Strong Will's love + caring new friends = earthly angels

#blessed

> *Earthly and heavenly angels are enfolding you with love and comfort. You are richly blessed.*
>
> —*Linda S*

> *Sometimes a rose is a rose, is a rose, is not really true. It is the significance with memories attached to it. Some things just carry a whole different meaning with what is attached. The love continues on in so many ways, does it not?*
>
> —*Louann*

Another Awareness

December 12, 2018

The Christmas cards have started to arrive. I didn't send as many this year. I've enjoyed making my own cards in the past but the creative energy isn't there right now.

Another year.

The envelopes caught me off guard. Addressed to me. *Just me.* I hadn't thought of that. When I signed cards that I sent, I signed my name. *Just mine......*more moments of "Oh, that's right."

I wrapped some gifts today, too. Like others, I save gift tags and sometimes reuse them. I found one that said "To Bill." Last year he received the gift attached to it. Last year he was here......last year.

Last year would be a welcome visitor.

There would still be time.

> *The holidays are great except when you are in grief and sorrow. Somehow the beauty of the season can make grieving even worse. Prayers for you that you get through it ok and even have some good moments to help you make it through.*
>
> —Sue

> *Every year for me, there is a moment of stillness where I experience the magnitude of the birth of Christ. Some years there are several moments like this. My prayer for you this year is that even in your grief, you will experience the joy of the season in some moment or several moments.*
>
> —Linda S

> *The happiest of seasons suddenly became the saddest. Sending prayers and love your way, knowing that once again you will be able to feel the love of Christmas.*
>
> —Diane

Christmas "Grieve"

December 24, 2018

As Christmas Eve settles into its last hour and we make ready for the morning, it's with the familiar feeling of sadness. When you know the heart of someone you love so well, you find yourself—even after they are gone— thinking, "I need to share this," discuss the music from a concert you've attended, bring him "up to date" on the latest news from friends. In the aftermath of these random realizations there is the emptiness. It's loud and long, an unending echo. So many moments in these last weeks were full of this awareness.

I've been grateful to have all of the kids— really our *adult* children—here. We've tried to make new memories and there has been lots of laughter. We're all being brave. Tonight both Zac and Jenn went to the Christmas Eve service with me looking exceptionally handsome and beautiful. I'm so proud. Aaron, home now, spent the evening celebrating Christmas with his mother and as I drift off to sleep I hear their vibrant young voices in the living room catching up on the day. Packages are under the tree for morning. Brunch will be ready. In the moments of time amid the bustle, I grieve—still wishing that someone else could be here with us.

> *Oh Marcia, it is stunning to me that you have been able to keep Bill so "alive" in so many ways to so many people. While I've gotten to know Bill through you in this journey, but I have gotten to know so much more about your strength and your ability to keep Bill a part of so many lives. It does not help you, that the physical piece is not here, but somehow, it seems that many of us have learned so much about the two of you as you have so kindly taken us along on your path to healing. All the best to all of you in this season and in the new year.*
>
> *—Louann*

> *I share your feelings. When we sang "Silent Night" at church last night I broke down. Christmas Eve was a special night and time for our family. But the person who I really want to wish Merry Christmas to is not here. He died at 1:20 a.m. the day after Christmas. I'm angry, hurt and sad that he is with his family in heaven having a very merry Christmas— and I am here alone. The day will pass - all too slowly - but it will pass and life goes on.*
>
> *—Luana*

With thoughts of peace and comfort for you as you continue on this journey with your amazing strength and God's hand guiding you. I pray the new year will be filled with blessings for all of you.

—Linda L

*The first Christmas without Bill here on earth after so many Christmases you had together. Something you neither anticipated nor expected. Unthinkable. And yet. All who love you want to take this pain away from you or experience it for you. Impossible. And yet. You **will** have the strength you need, you **will** do the grieving that you must do and need to do. And we will stand with you lending our strength, our prayers, and our love and grieving him, too.*

—Linda S

Peace

December 25, 2018

A quiet day—but lovely. We had a brunch and gift exchange this morning. Aaron left for Grand Rapids to spend time with girlfriend Deb's family while Zac and Jenn spent the rest of the day with me which was special. We went to a silly movie and then had dinner back here. Tonight it's quiet. Zac leaves in the morning but we're enjoying the Christmas tree lights and conversation. These, too, are precious moments to savor.

Life.
Love.
Family.
Peace.

Bill was with us today. Each of the kids has a tangible part of him now—hand blown glass paperweights with his ashes sparkling inside to represent his light and goodness. We can hold these treasures with love.

> *What a beautiful gift!*
>
> *—Claudia*

> *Some things are just perfect. Nuff said.*
>
> *—Linda S*

"We've Got You!"

December 30, 2018

Despite the sadness of this journey there are beautiful moments along the way. I continue to feel gratitude for those who care and reach out in support. In church last Sunday I fell apart during the closing hymn. Suddenly, two women joined me on either side wrapping an arm around me and softly whispered, "We've got you!" We stood in a little threesome gently swaying to the music as the song finished. There was unspeakable comfort in that small period of time—yet another blessing. ("Amazing grace! How sweet the sound that saved a wretch like me..." Yes.)

I'm in Chicago now visiting sister Linda and husband Steve. Their warmth and welcoming kindness is so special. Son Zac is nearby, too, and we spent yesterday together. What gifts these relationships are—always, of course—but especially right now. I often wonder how people without faith cope. God's grace presents itself through the love of these people in our lives. I've said it before and it bears repeating: earthly angels are watching over me.

So blessed.

> *The Lord will never leave us to cope on our own. His love for us is beyond our understanding. I, too, cannot understand how people cope without faith. Prayers and hugs to you. Take care.*
>
> *—Cherryl*

> *I'm so glad that you have the right people at the right time to give what you need. I know that your upcoming anniversary will not be easy. Prayers for you to get through that day. Larry's cousin also lost her battle with pancreatic cancer. As we were at her service yesterday, I couldn't help but think of you and Bill. She had been scheduled to go through another particularly awful round of chemo. Her pastor asked her if she was sure that she wanted to and she said, "Yes, I want to stand and fight." I thought of you and Bill and all of your standing and fighting. One comforting thing the pastor said is that her light has been passed on to each one of us whose lives she touched. It's certainly true of Bill also. His light has been passed onto each person he knew and especially to you and through you.*
>
> *—Sue*

> *Your writings are thoughtful meditations for us all. May family, friends, and faith continue to bless and support you on this arduous journey.*
>
> *—Julie S*

A New Year

January 1, 2019

Yesterday, New Year's Eve, would have been our 22nd wedding anniversary. I wonder if anniversaries still exist once your partner passes away. Am I still part of a couple? A marriage? We joked that getting married on New Year's Eve was really poor planning— it's so hard to get a dinner reservation. We liked it being celebratory and Bill joked it was great tax planning, too— getting married on the last day of the year. We had many funny and sweet moments around the decision to make December 31 our wedding date. Now it feels hollow. Now I'd happily struggle to get a reservation somewhere. It would mean he's still here.

Last night at my sister's in Chicago, we went to a party at the neighbors. It was a really lovely and welcoming group of people. All couples. And me.

Today a new year began—one Bill did not live to experience. So again, another awareness: here I am. 2019 without Strong Will. How many other moments will surface like these?

I'm so sorry that your anniversary date is one that others are celebrating while you are struggling. Bravo for you for putting on a good face and attending a party while hurting. The year ahead will not be "easy" in any sense of the word, but many prayers go with you that you will find some kind of blessing each day.

—Sue

New Year's Eve was a special day for me too as 45 years ago on New Year's Eve was my first "blind" date with soon to be husband Rick. What a date that was! There are still sad times, but I know there is a lot of celebrating going on for Rick and Bill – they are so happy with no illness or pain. The Lord is guiding us here and will never leave us in 2019 or ever. Take care and Hugs!

—Cherryl

You were so courageous to go out on New Year's Eve. That was such a positive action, and also there is nothing like the support of a loving sister. You are finding your way through this difficult time, although you may not feel it. Bill is proud of you,

—Diane

Trail of Tears

January 18, 2019

I've dubbed the route to Beaumont Hospital "The Trail of Tears". So many trips were under great duress and worry throughout the last year. I reread the journal entry from exactly one year ago where Bill was halfway through his chemo treatments. We just didn't know how the next eight months would go and maybe that's for the best— because we had hope. We kept praying and striving to do all we could to battle that awful cancer. Our prayers didn't waiver and we stayed the course.

Today I drove that route to Beaumont reflecting on all those many months; but today it was for my mammogram. Very routine. Yet as I approached the hospital campus so many memories flooded my thoughts. Bill had such good care and the very best treatment they could offer. But God had a different plan— one that left me with great sadness and the challenge to trust that His comfort and care will sustain me. That's where I must put my faith. And you know what? It *is* a little better. "Living and doing" keep me centered on being positive. After my exam, I met a friend for lunch—one of the "angels" I met during the time we spent in the area. This wonderful woman was responsible for the great accommodations at the hotel near the hospital. She was so helpful and made sure every stay was perfect. She has become a friend and this is one of those blessings I've shared in previous journal entries.

Last week, Jenn and I went to south Florida—where Bill and I spent so many vacations. My sister Linda joined us for a few days and we made some happy, new memories. While it was bittersweet to experience so many familiar spots without Bill, I didn't feel a terrible longing for him. I felt the joy of many happy memories we shared there together— and they fused with the new ones. It will never, ever be the same just as I will never, ever be the same— but I know this gradual path is one I must take. No one can do it for me. No one can fix it or diminish the grief. It's the love of God and the treasured people in my life who help ease what I must do.

> *Your very thoughtful posts continue to amaze and inform, Marcia. Finding gratitude through this journey is a true blessing. Prayers for continued strength.*
>
> *—Julie S*

You were and still are so loved! So glad you have stayed in touch with your angels along the way.

—Cindy H

You give a voice to so many who have been and/or are in your circumstances: the good, the bad, and the ugly, Thank you. You are a blessing.

—Linda S

This I Know

When someone you love dies, it's beyond horrible. No matter how much "warning" you get, the devastation is surreal. It's pain. Immense sadness. Loneliness without comparison. Grief is an unwelcome visitor every day.

But this I know:

The devastating grip begins to ease.
Slowly.
Gradually.

It's a subtle awareness that the deep ache inside is a *little* less deep. Getting through the day is less insurmountable. Most importantly, it's knowing God is present as we make our way. We are not alone. Ever. His unconditional love is present no matter how badly we falter. We can find comfort being with others: at church, social gatherings, accepting (and extending) invitations, or connecting through a phone call. It's our obligation to welcome that outreach—even when it's hard. On the other side of it, we do begin to feel peace. A breath of life— though new and different. It's our challenge as these "wounded healers" to share it with others who will walk this path. Their journey may be new or time may have passed and they've become stuck. But isn't it a joy to think we *might* have an impact in some small way to help our brothers and sisters in Christ become "unstuck"?

I think so.

> *You are right on point, dear friend, grieving and healing. Years ago when my mother was in her 80's, she told me that she still missed her mother. She said that it hurt her that her mom never got to see her great grandson's birth. I hugged her and said a very stupid thing. I said, "After all these years, I am surprised that you are still grieving your mother—my grandma." She replied, "Well it isn't a real sharp pain anymore, but it is still a deep, dull ache." Now I know from experience what she was trying to teach me—and for what she was trying to prepare me.*
>
> *—Linda S*

Marcia you have a gift of explaining this process so well. It's exactly how I feel after the love of my life passed on to our heavenly home 18 months ago. Bless you! As hard as it is, it's good to know you are moving along in this unknown process. Hugs and love.

—*Pam L*

Because of what you have been through and continue to feel, your feelings have given you the gift to pass on to others as some have done for you. While it is you, right here, that is doing the passing, if it were not for Bill, and your struggle with him in his illness, and your life with him, you would not be able to do what you are doing for others. Also, never forget that your acceptance of the love, calls, etc. are another way that you are giving- allowing others in your life.

—*Louann*

Epilogue

The decision to publish Bill's story was an easy one. There was so much to share about his courage and strength and determination. A diagnosis of pancreatic cancer is so terrifying and yet, there is always hope. From the feedback I received from those who followed our story on Caring Bridge© to those I met along the way, everyone held that same hope and voiced encouragement. There is a story to tell, they said. We held fast to the strong desire that this would result in a cure. And sometimes it does—or delays what may be inevitable. As recently as March of 2019, the news reported there is a new blood test promising earlier detection. People of fame and people of modest means face this dreaded diagnosis. Cancer is a leavening agent unlike any other. We face it wherever we are in life. Dr. Douglas Evans told us he had never met a person with this diagnosis who was not a wonderful human being. His zest for knowing patients at this level brings great comfort to those of us who have this cancer or are their loved ones. We cling to the humanity and stripped-away-to-the-bone rawness of being in this moment. Yet, without hope and faith, continuing is insurmountable. Relying on those who can help carry the load eases the burden. Many reach out and touch us along the way. We must be open to this kindness, the loving acts, and willing to accept the gifts when it may not be easy. The benefits of the reciprocity are great, healing, and precious.

We were so fortunate to have so many supporters. Family and friends were there for us…in presence, in phone calls, in communication on the website. Bill received many gifts: a handmade plate by niece Mackenzie with "Strong Will" scripted across its decorative surface, a prayer shawl from our church, cozy cabin socks from Aaron's friend, a fleece lined MSU hat to warm him on chilly days traveling to the hospital for treatment, a favorite Irish whisky from another friend of Aaron's, a clever light up sign proclaiming our battle cry, "Strong Will" from Jenn, fresh flowers "just because," plants and green touches to make our away home feel more like a real home, communion on Sunday evenings from a new Wisconsin friend, Liz, and the list goes on. It really isn't about "stuff," though. It's the thought that goes into these special gifts. It says, "I care about you." Gratitude flows when we are the recipients of moments like these. We have hope, we experience terrible losses, we grieve, but we have loved. And the love carries us to new places of comfort.

That is the essence of life and our reason for being on this earth.

—Marcia, Strong Will's wife

ACKNOWLEDGMENTS

While this book is a love story about a wonderful man, it is also about gratitude. There are many people to thank who impacted, supported, and simply loved us through this journey. It's almost impossible to grow spiritually without understanding sacrifice and pain. I believe some of what I've taken away is that we are loved even in great and trying times, but the shielding factor is the love of God and those He puts in our path to care about us physically.

Thank you, Dr. Margolis, Dr. Evans, and Dr. Erickson for your skill and compassion. Thank you to our incredible children, Zac, Jenn, and Aaron and girlfriend, Deb who continue to love me and remember Bill in the very best of ways. Thank you to our extended families— siblings Linda Coen (our lucky cricket) and husband Steve, Amy Miller and husband Dan, Carolyn Kik and husband Jim, Sam Wright and wife Cathy, Tom Wright and wife Robine, Bill's mother, Rita Wright and nieces Mackenzie Coen, Cassie Wright, Chelsea Wright, Amy Sommers and nephews Bill Kik, Jim Kik, and Riley Miller who all "showed up" with love in their hearts. Two other nephews, Dillon Miller and Jonathan Coen were unable to be with us but we were grateful for their prayers. I'm forever grateful to Sheryl Jackson who arranged perfect lodging for us during Bill's Michigan hospitalizations and chemotherapy days.

Thank you to our home community-dear neighbors and friends, Bob and Cindy Melnik, Pastor Drew Hart, Pastor Chris Brundage, Julie Shultz, Lora Crombez, Jean Thurman, Jim Caldwell from the prayer team. Thank you to all of the Caring Bridge© supporters who fell into multiple supportive categories and offered encouragement, prayers, and insightful words—Louann Edwards, Linda and Jim Sanborn, Sally Rae, Luana Bixler, Barbara Foor, Diane Adams, Cheryll Leonard, Dianna Raine, Sue Ries, Dawn Clark, Cherryl Jackson, Gretchen Knapp, Carol Wahl, Ginny Weeks, Margaret Dickerson, Sally Powers, Carrie Clark, Lisa Nation, Esther Carr, Debbie Langmeyer, Barb and Gary Dawes, Pam LeForge, Shannon Rodriguez, Marvin and Claudia Sauer, Dody Robertson, Don Fry, Lisa Doty, Lynne Olsen, Keith Spaulding, Jan Parson, Brandon Farver, Justin and Allie Potes, Zach Hammer, Linda Lentner, Mary Kemerer, Donna Nelson, Sheila Polley, Laura VanSickle, Debbie Brighton, Darlene Frederick, Kathy Selman, Marcia Lengnick, Julie Jones, Todd and Jackie Dunbar, Linda Wagner, Karen Perez, Lynn Olsen, Valerie Wilson, Kris Tomczak, Pam Price, Mitzy Menzer, Kay Doyle, Stephanie

Carlton, Joyce Collins, Sharon Weber, Jan Haines, Cindy Howard, Mary Ann Lysaght, Mary Maxe, Nancy Miller, Nancy Howe, Nancy Borchard, Marla Erickson, and so many more. Bill's longtime dear friend, Dave Selman traveled all the way from south Florida to see him while we were in Wisconsin-a visit that was so special. Along with unfailing support, another friend, Sherm Shultz brought Bill reading material, fun gifts, and cheerful news to distract him before, during, and after treatment. While in Wisconsin, Liz Berlyn became a friend through the P.E.O. chapter who welcomed me as a visiting member and brought communion to Bill. Frank and Linda Roberts, also Michigan natives, whose journey mirrored ours, became lasting friends. We were grateful, too, for the frequent books, packages, and fresh flowers from family and friends back home.

As Bill's illness and passing grew more imminent, my former colleagues and friends from Clinton Elementary School organized meals as did my local P.E.O. sisters. Amy Jo Walters, who catered our wedding brunch 22 years ago, delivered food to our home that lasted for days. Rita Adams, yogi and dear friend, cycled many miles with Bill and then rode in his memory.

Grief Share© offered support after Bill died. The bonds formed with facilitators Rene and Lora Crombez, Brian Bowers, and Jean Thurman along with participants Ellen Anderson, Rhea Stephens, Liz Jarrell, and Michelle Cook, and Linda Barker formed a precious connection. Grief Share© program locations can be found online (www.griefshare.org) and are offered all over the country with a mission to help those experiencing loss cope. Finally, this list, while undoubtedly incomplete, must include Pat Stafford Sturk, who supported us via Caring Bridge©, phone calls, visits, and deserves an additional and *huge* thank you for her editing and proofreading skills. What a woman!

And so I go on- learning to live differently each day. What I thought would be a predictable life is far from that. But each day is a gift and an opportunity to show gratitude.

Thank you for reading our story.